T0311743

Cambridge Elements

Elements in the Global Middle Ages
edited by
Geraldine Heng
University of Texas at Austin
Susan Noakes
University of Minnesota, Twin Cities

CAHOKIA AND THE NORTH AMERICAN WORLDS

Sarah E. Baires
Eastern Connecticut State University

CAMBRIDGE
UNIVERSITY PRESS

CAMBRIDGE
UNIVERSITY PRESS

University Printing House, Cambridge CB2 8BS, United Kingdom

One Liberty Plaza, 20th Floor, New York, NY 10006, USA

477 Williamstown Road, Port Melbourne, VIC 3207, Australia

314–321, 3rd Floor, Plot 3, Splendor Forum, Jasola District Centre,
New Delhi – 110025, India

103 Penang Road, #05–06/07, Visioncrest Commercial, Singapore 238467

Cambridge University Press is part of the University of Cambridge.

It furthers the University's mission by disseminating knowledge in the pursuit of
education, learning, and research at the highest international levels of excellence.

www.cambridge.org
Information on this title: www.cambridge.org/9781108928762
DOI: 10.1017/9781108934077

First published 2022

A catalogue record for this publication is available from the British Library.

ISBN 978-1-108-92876-2 Paperback
ISSN 2632-3427 (online)
ISSN 2632-3419 (print)

Cahokia and the North American Worlds

Elements in the Global Middle Ages

DOI: 10.1017/9781108934077
First published online: February 2022

Sarah E. Baires
Eastern Connecticut State University

Author for correspondence: Sarah E. Baires, bairess@easternct.edu

Abstract: The city of Cahokia provides a unique case study to review what draws people to the place and why. This Element examines not only the emergence and decline of this great American city but also its intersection with the broader Native American world during medieval period. Cahokia was not an isolated complex but a place vivid on the landscape where people made pilgrimages to and from Cahokia for trade and religious practices. It was a central place with expansive reach and cultural influence. This Element analyzes the social and political processes that helped create this city while also reflecting on the trajectory of Native American history in North America.

Keywords: Native North America, Cahokia, temporalities, historicity, city

ISBNs: 9781108928762 (PB), 9781108934077 (OC)
ISSNs: 2632-3427 (online), 2632-3419 (print)

Contents

1 Introduction

Imagining a city recalls noise, congested streets, buildings reaching upward, neighborhoods, and networks of relationships. Cities, from a Western perspective, structure the human experience (De Certeau 2011). Urban sites unite the American (and global) panorama as nodes in a series of relationships: economic, social, religious, and agricultural. The city is a vibrant landscape, constructed not only by the buildings and infrastructure that create its visceral history but also by the persons (human and other-than-human) who populate its spaces. From this perspective, the city is alive and is a place of creation. This "aliveness" is performative and embodied in the city's struggle to grow, create, and thrive where persons navigate the intimate connections among place, history, and experience through the material and experiential expression of thought and interaction. As archaeological relics, cities constitute places of the knowable past whereby investigation into the debris of everyday life – its infrastructure, public spaces, minutia of home life – creates historical narratives. Cities developed independently all over the globe beginning in the fourth millennium BCE drawing diverse persons into permanent settlements that "crystallized independently all over the planet" (see Yoffee 2015: 3). Early cities grew as points of pilgrimage, ceremony, and trade and exchange; religious and cultural centers; and places for politics and defense. Archaeology is fascinated by early cities; research questions range from, for example, why humans chose to move from isolated farmsteads, small towns, and rural hamlets into proximity with one another, to considering the benefits of this type of living. Cities seemingly became the new social imaginary whereby community practices worked to make sense of cultural, political, and social relationships experienced through the built landscape.

This Element is an examination of the processes of city creation and urbanization in pre-Columbian North America with a particular focus on Cahokia – the preeminent Native American city, north of the Rio Grande river. Cahokia was part of a unique assemblage of Indigenous central places that characterize the Middle Ages in the Eastern Woodlands in the North American midcontinent (Figure 1). These places are identified by earthen mounds, public plazas, and thatch-roofed houses organized into neighborhoods and small communities and the nearby agricultural fields or small garden plots supplying food to the community. Early Native American urban places were arranged by the physical spaces of the landscape and by the material embodiment of human and other-than-human interaction, resulting in the pottery, stone tools, textiles, figurines, basketry, and other objects that form social life. Drawing from the rich archaeological data of the region, I trace the emergence of the city of Cahokia to

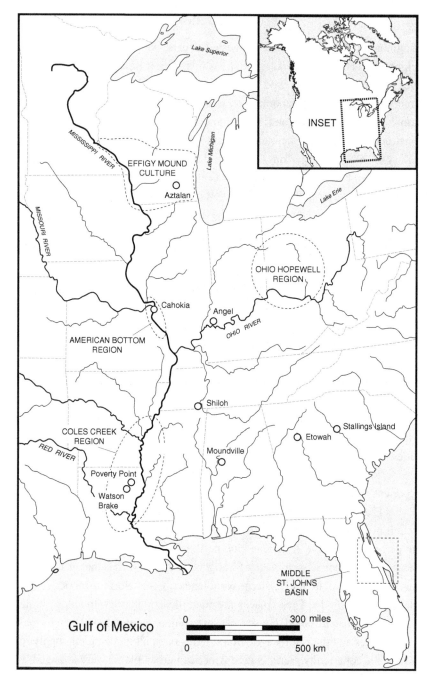

Figure 1 Map of the Eastern Woodlands with archaeological sites discussed in the text (base map courtesy of Tim Pauketat)

its decline, contextualizing this city within the broader network of Native American sites and histories in the Eastern Woodlands. Throughout this examination, I consider the ways in which the Native American past becomes historicized *as well as* the ways in which the Indigenous experience is subsumed by the colonial European history of the United States. To accomplish this, I explore how Cahokia's rich past shapes the contemporary experience and interpretation of this early city. This analysis reflects the process of history creation and for whom it is created (see Stewart 2016: 81; see also Todd 2016).

An anthropological perspective brings a unique lens to historicity – one that focuses on the diversity of experience while emphasizing the cultural context from which past experience originates (see Ohnuki-Tierney 1990). Historicity is about "the relationship of being to time" constituted by an individual connection to the past established from the present (Stewart 2016: 80). In anthropological archaeology, an understanding of history must be widened to include the diverse ways persons relate to and perceive the past, as well as its representation (Stewart 2016; see also Papailias 2005). This is particularly salient when discussing history and time from an Indigenous point of view. Deloria Jr. (1973) emphasizes that temporalities (and histories) are place- and context-based; time as something linear (progressing from past to future) does not exist. Humans and other-than-human persons experience their world as part of assemblages of matter and place; this is where histories emerge as traceable networks of interconnected parts accessible in the present through the ruins of the past (see Ingold 1993: 157). Time and history are composed of events, persons, landscapes, and processes that defy a linear projection. Histories, therefore, can be experienced as ever-present aspects of social life contributing to the ways persons reimagine and recreate their world through practice.

The intimacy of history, or the ways historical moments invade and populate present spaces, is part of being in the world and serves as a catalyst for a person's participation in creating cultural relationships (see Stewart 2016). These relationships are not fixed. There is no past, present, and future as sequentially ordered (see Heidegger 1953 [1996]); human and other-than-human experience of the world is predicated upon the experiential conditions of self in relation to others – other places, other persons, other moments, and other events. Thinking of temporality and even history as interconnected moments that permeate all aspects of social life rather than a linear progression from past to future allows for infinite possibilities of experience. Yet, in a discipline (i.e., archaeology) whose sole purpose is to excavate, analyze, and theorize "the past," how do we take this "blurring" of time seriously? Furthermore, how do we bring that concept into analyses very much situated within a structured past/present/future?

Archaeology is a social science concerned with the past and its impact upon the future. Analyses are built upon a linear progression of time that involves the categorization of places and objects into temporally bound types. These "types" are arranged into broader categories of similar things that build our understanding of the past. Types are further constituted by trait lists and stylistic markers that work to "decode" the past, thus ordering it into geographical and temporal categories of human culture. Archaeological inquiry is about collecting material evidence of the prehistoric and historic past "in pursuit of a broad and comprehensive understanding of human culture" (Society for American Archaeology "What is Archaeology" https://www.saa.org/about-archaeology/what-is-archae ology accessed March 2020). In the very definition of archaeology is the word "history" broken into segments that designate a time before written documentation (pre) and a time after humans began to write down their pasts (history).

But, in the Americas, this designation goes a bit further to classify the Indigenous inhabitants of the North American continent as "freaks outside historical time" (Deloria 1992: 597; see also Irwin 1994; Kolodny 2003). Deloria's critique of how archaeologists designate time periods based on the so-called discovery of North America by Columbus brings up a salient issue in archaeology – one that concerns the epistemological understanding of history. The added designation of "pre" to discuss all Native American historical experiences prior to the arrival of Europeans violently slashes through the record of human existence on this continent separating Native Americans from Euro-Americans. This separation created the basis for the future expansionist narrative of the American dream – Manifest Destiny – where the "vanishing Indian" (devoid of recorded history) was removed from the landscape in an attempt at cultural erasure (see Baires 2017a, 2020; Martinez 2006; Turner 1894). This designation of prehistory denotes an idea of "lesser than," where Indigenous histories become relegated to the unwritten and therefore speculative past. From this perspective, archaeologists became the authority of this ("pre")history, creating a narrative of the North American continent prior to European contact framed from Enlightenment thought (see Deloria 1992; Todd 2016; Watts 2013b). For many, the archaeological framework predicated on the divide between "historic" and "pre" served a useful function: it allowed for the unfettered analysis and treatment of Native American persons as data points (see Pauketat 2013a for critique). Much critique has been leveled at this approach (see Pauketat 2002), arguing that human agency, among other things, was missing from this type of analysis. Gaining steam in the 1980s and 1990s, the post-processual movement laid the foundation for a new way of thinking about and examining history in archaeology – one that became concerned with what trait lists and cultural histories *can say* about the human experience through examinations of materiality, gender, postcolonialism, and practice. This movement also ushered in collaborative archaeological studies (see, e.g., Atalay 2012; Silliman 2008) and later more progressive analyses of the archaeological record concerned with alternate ways of being – the ontological turn.

The ontological turn in archaeology can be marked by the introduction of the work of Bruno Latour (1993, 2005) and later by Eduardo Viveiros de Castro (2012, 2014; see Alberti 2016) who seemingly pushed archaeologists beyond the epistemological questions of the processual and even post-processual movements to consider the relational aspects of humans and other-than-human persons. The ontological approach in archaeology is built upon the "material turn" and a concern for things as well as an emphasis on phenomenological experiences of the landscape (see Jones and Alberti 2013; Olsen 2012; Watts 2013a). This focus on the materiality and experiential qualities of human social life began to "reconfigure archaeology theoretically and conceptually on the basis of indigenous theory" (Alberti 2016: 164; see also Alberti and Marshall 2009; Fowles 2013). In archaeology, "ontology" either refers to "reality itself 'what there is' (Fowler 2013: 61) or people's claims about reality, 'a fundamental set of understanding about how the world is'" (Alberti 2016: 165). This sort of framework, and the one that takes Indigenous theoretical perspectives seriously (see Kimmerer 2013; Povinelli 2016; Todd 2016; Watts 2013b), "revisits the way(s) in which – or by which – the world actually exists" (Alberti et al. 2011: 897).

What the ontological turn can offer an archaeology of Native North America is its emphasis on the pluralistic nature of ontologies as well as the social and agentic aspect of the material world (see Haraway 2007; Olsen 2010; Thomas 2015). Objects and pieces of matter, places, humans, and other-than-human persons are constituted by their relations, which are always in a state of becoming (Barad 2003; see also Alberti and Marshall 2009; Ingold 2015; Jones 2012).

These sets of relations (or assemblages [following Deleuze and Guattari 1988]) suggest an "openness rather than closure" – or a *dynamic* cultural system (see Alberti 2016: 167; see also Fowler 2013). This "openness" requires that archaeology consider the relational qualities of human and other-than-human participants where assemblages of matter (things, persons, and places) make up the social world (see Barad 2003; see also Baires 2020). This is central to the study of Native American history whereby the material components of the living world *can be* agents in their own right (see Baires 2017a, 2020; Pauketat 2013a). This perspective recognizes that social realities are constituted by multiple actors, not all of whom are human, making these realities "ripe with sites of potentiality" (Zigon 2015: 504; see also Baires 2020; Harris 2018; Olsen 2010). It is through these interactions and their potentialities that histories develop in the present – meaning histories, too, are always in a state of becoming (à la Barad 2003); they are multitemporal (Fowler 2013: 242–245; see also Hamilakis 2013; Olsen 2010). While the designations of "past" and "history" aid in the organization of human social experience from a Western ontological view, it must be recognized that these same designations may muddle the experiential aspects of non-Western realities. A relational ontological framework requires a recognition of difference that takes the "otherness" of materials seriously to better understand the relationships created between nonhumans and humans (see Pe'tursdo'ttir and Olsen 2014). These relationships are the "stuff" of human and other-than-human experiences *and* histories, which are accessible in the present through analyses of how the recursive relationship between past and contemporary cultural contexts shapes meaning. Archaeological sites present a unique case to examine this "otherness" as these places exist in multiple temporalities: as past realities and contemporary ruins.

Cahokia: Archaeological City and Contemporary Ruin

The idea that the past is never quite in the past influences the ways one may think about and relate to places like Cahokia. This Native American city lives in multiple realities. Cahokia was the cultural behemoth of the pre-Columbian Midwest: a monumental Native American city occupied from c. CE 1050 to CE 1400 constituted by three sprawling precincts connected across the Mississippi River in southern Illinois (Figure 2). Furthermore, this place had its own history

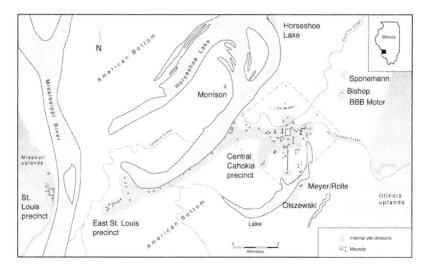

Figure 2 Map of the city of Cahokia: East St. Louis, St. Louis, and Cahokia precincts (map courtesy of Tim Pauketat)

built upon a series of Indigenous realities going back to the Archaic period traditions of earthmoving and mound building at sites like Poverty Point, Louisiana (see Section 3). These traditions were constructed out of and into the earth, where the built environment tells the stories of its human and other-than-human occupants through terraforming (or human modification of the land for habitation [see Randall and Sassaman 2017]) and the careful layering of soils into mounds. At Cahokia, decades of cultural resource management archaeology, Works Progress Administration projects, and academic investigations provide ample evidence that this urban landscape was populated by upward of 40,000 people (bringing with them their own histories) (see Benson et al. 2009; Brennan 2018; Pauketat and Lopinot 1997), some immigrants, some local, who upon taking up residence in this city adopted its planned neighborhoods, pottery styles, and cultural narratives. To be "Cahokian" meant living your life in a particular way (see Pauketat 2004, 2013a for summaries). This is not to suggest that Cahokia lacked diversity (see Alt 2002, 2018; Emerson and Hedman 2016; Slater et al. 2014), but rather to emphasize that Cahokia was like any other urban place – its people were joined together by a shared way of being manifested materially in pots, projectile points, house construction, food choices, and earthmoving. This reality is superimposed by a contemporary Cahokia, a site crisscrossed by modern highways, bounded by farmlands; a drive-through liquor stores; middle- and lower-class neighborhoods; immigrant-owned restaurants; and abandoned, boarded-up buildings (Figure 3). Once you cross the boundary into the state historic site – marked by a wooden sign – you experience the ruins of a once living, breathing, and thriving city seemingly bridging the arbitrary divide between past and present.

Ruins, often depicted as frozen in time, consist of monumental structures, perhaps with overgrown landscapes and crumbling exteriors. In the popular narrative, a ruin is romantic, coveted by colonial enterprises and explorers seeking ties to the past through the legacies of spectacular places. According to Dawdy (2010 [citing Murray 2008]), "cycles of ruin, destruction and abandonment are a defining feature of cities" – multilayered phenomena built and rebuilt on the remnants of the past. The transformation from the active site to ruin is contingent upon (1) a process of othering and (2) how much time has passed. Ancient ruins are places whose histories become romanticized where the ancient ruin nestled among the modern landscape becomes a place of heritage value composed of an "aesthetically pleasing and monumental" site "promoting certain western-elite cultural conceptions and values" (Pe'tursdo'ttir 2013: 34). The ancient ruin becomes an attraction; it is heritage, a nonrenewable resource to be protected (however, see Dawdy's [2010] discussion of modern ruin voyeurism), and a place that remains the same through time.

Figure 3 Cahokia Mounds State Park and adjacent mobile home neighborhood, Collinsville, Illinois

This "sameness" creates a romantic nostalgia sought when visited by tourists and community members alike.

At Cahokia Mounds State Historic Site, ancient ruins literally overlap with the contemporary urban landscape (e.g., modern buildings located atop partially bulldozed mounds) and create a palimpsest of matter and time. The process of ruination lies in the place where the two temporalities meet, which is at once a mental space and a material place (see Smith 2006). The materiality of ruins is characterized by their meanings where differential interpretations of places can influence things like identity, access, and use. Their context of creation is also important here; narratives of "ownership" constructed from historical processes like dispossession and colonialism linger on the landscape structuring the ways persons use and view spaces. To ruin is often a political process and, in the context of the settler-colonial landscape of North America, is entangled with the dispossession of non-Western, non-white persons from their lands – both ancestral and contemporary. Settler colonialism, like colonialism, is "premised on exogenous domination, but only settler colonialism *seeks to replace the original population of the colonized territory with a new society of settlers*" (LeFevre 2015: 1, emphasis added). This desire stems from a need for land and territory and a need to stay on that land; as Wolfe (2006: 288) states, "invasion is a structure not an event." In America, settler colonialism focused on "a protypical American 'self' (i.e., 'the American Adam'), on a specific quest (i.e., 'the errand into the wilderness'), and on the process of acquisition/liberation of the land (i.e., 'a virgin land') against all sort of indigenous and exogenous challenges" (Veracini 2013: 324). The central workings of settler colonialism hinge upon the distinction of Native American tribes as sovereign nations situated on the frontiers of expanding colonial empires. European settlers who were the first to appear on sovereign Indian land had the right to claim and acquire that land on behalf of their own sovereign. Native peoples had the right to sell "their" land to the settler, but "[t]he American right to buy always superseded the Indian right to sell" (Wolfe 2006: 391). There was no choice for the American Indian.

The makings of the United States by balking against European colonial control created a unique state where new Americans sought resistance to their colonialization by colonizing others (Hoxie 2008). Indigenous North American identity was entangled with the land, and as such, white settlers viewed the American Indians as obstacles to what they coveted, but the Native Americans also connected new Americans to a sense of history –albeit one that was not their own (Deloria 1988, 2003). Land and territory, for new Americans, embodied the American ideology of exploration and conquering the wilderness. Through this process of conquering, Indigenous peoples fell to multiple affronts on their communities. Religious conversion, child abduction, missions and boarding schools, violence, and the reorganization of native lands into individual plots available for claim buoyed the white Euro-American goal of "destroy to replace" (see Wolfe 2006: 388–389). Yet these processes did not negate the periods of alliances and negotiated peace between the two groups. These moments, however fleeting, created settler nations where new Americans and the Indians "gradually came to share languages, family ties, religious faiths, economies, political systems, and common popular culture" (Hoxie 2008: 1159). Indigenous traditions persisted, but the expansion of the settler states continued to work to replace and displace "deficient" Indigenous communities (see Deloria 1988; Hoxie 2008; Wolfe 2006; see also Silliman 2005).

One of the ways this settler history manifested was through the Moundbuilder Myth, which plagued America during the nineteenth century and can be summarized as the coveting of Native American ruins by the people of Euro-American descent. This covetousness hinged on the idea that the grassy knolls that crisscrossed the midcontinent were products of some lost race who traveled to the Americas, built the mounds and presumably the cities they were part of, and were later run out by the "savage Indian" (see Howey 2012). This thinking spurred a Victorian nostalgia that emphasized the settler colonial need to be tied to place – to identify one's own heritage in the occupied landscape (see Maile 2017).

Through a co-optation of Moundbuilder landscapes, settlers shirked the legitimate claims Native American communities put forth about these lands and worked instead to create their own narrative of ownership. They did this effectively by harkening back to ideas of Old World peoples who, in their mind, must have inhabited the Americas before Native Americans and built these monumental earthworks. This idea, in the mind of the settlers, legitimized European colonization and placed themselves in the Americas prior to the arrival of the Indians (see Arjona 2015; Howey 2012). This was in part supported by William Bartram's recordings of local Native American accounts of the mounds, which seemingly corroborated their mythical origins. According to Bartram's early journals (*Travels*, originally published in 1791), the Creek and the Cherokee, for example, who lived around such mounds, attributed their construction to "the ancients, many ages prior to their arrival and possessing of this country." Bartram's account of Creek and Cherokee histories led to the view that these Native Americans were colonizers, just like Euro-Americans. The Moundbuilder Myth sanctioned settler need to claim lands west of the original colonies; it provided another justification for the continued removal and displacement of the Native Americans. The logic went that if Native Americans did not build those mounds but the ancient Greeks or some other Western society did, then the settlers have just as much of a right to that land as the Native Americans because it was their ancestors who were here first.

While the Moundbuilder narrative was deconstructed by archaeologists in the late nineteenth and early twentieth centuries (see Trigger 1980 for an overview), the legacy of this settler ideology remains in the co-optation of Indigenous spaces and ruins by people of Euro-American descent. This co-optation manifests in multiple ways from the literal paving over of Indigenous sites to the transformation of archaeological ruins into state-owned or federally owned parks and monuments. This settler-colonial context of early America is pertinent here because this history constructs how researchers and tourists experience and engage with Indigenous ruins and sites like Cahokia. It shapes the types of research conducted, the narratives produced, and the site protections put in place. It also shapes how we understand Cahokia as part of (and perhaps stuck in) the past – a place to be looked upon as a relic where "historians narrate the 'story' of indigenous people in North America in the shadow of these trends" (see Hoxie 2008: 1154). To reframe this narrative, analyses must consider Cahokia as not only "of the past" but also "of the present," where the city's role in social life did not end with its so-called decline c. 1350 CE (see Baltus 2014 for an alternate narrative). This brings back the conceptualization of temporalities as permeable whereby movements of persons may create "discontinuous experiences" structured by "the contours of history by challenging the familiar and extrapolating the space of experience onto horizons of expectations" (Sassaman 2016: 275). In the context of Cahokia, place and time are linked whereby memories, relationships, and movements become social knowledge in the "*space of experience, in which past things are present or can be remembered*" (Sassaman 2016: 276; see also Koselleck 2004). This "type" of history, the one based on the experiential aspects of human and other-than-human relations, creates a place ripe with potentialities. Those potentialities are not bounded by a sense of past, present, and future, but rather flow through shared experiences working to create new futures.

Cahokia, at once both the vibrant Native American city and the archaeological ruin situated in the contemporary urban landscape of Collinsville, Illinois, creates a unique context to examine this interlocking of past and present futures. The grass-covered earthen mounds, the footprints of thatch-roofed houses and storage pits, burials mounds, and plaza spaces conjure a sense of nostalgia and historicity (or the culturally conditioned ways a particular history is understood [Ohnuki-Tierney 1990]), which must be addressed when revisiting Cahokia as a place of the past. Yet this place is also alive with the movements of its inhabitants who built the mounds, lived in and used the thatch-roofed houses and storage pits, buried their dead, and gathered in the plazas. To understand something or someplace as only "of-the-past" facilitates the continuation of artificial temporal divisions that create and sustain colonial narratives about human cultural experience and development. The question must then become, how do we move beyond those boundaries without muddying the waters of academic analysis *and* cultural memory? Framing a "past" experience within the context of movements may help create a sense of time not bounded by divisions. Drawing from Ingold (1993: 162), movements and performances generate the "taskscape" of human (and other-than-human) experience and its relationship to the landscape where neither is truly ever "complete." Both spaces, as interrelated and interactive aspects of social life, are "perpetually under construction" (Ingold 1993). Humans, other-than-humans, and the landscape are entangled "where time is a turning circle … a place where prophecy and history converge" (Kimmerer 2013: 207). Applying this concept of fluid temporality emphasizes that knowledge (or histories) is also entangled with the land. The land, then, becomes a permeable space where past, present, and future experiences are accessible simultaneously (again see Kimmerer 2013 on Indigenous temporalities).

Coming back to Cahokia, a contemporary ruin and a (pre)historic thriving city, these concepts of taskscapes, permeable landscapes, and cyclical temporalities are reminders that nothing is truly ever of the past, but rather reexperienced in dynamic ways. Even after Cahokia becomes "abandoned" (but see Baltus 2014; White et al. 2020), persons continue to live on that landscape, travel to and by this city, and recall/reexperience it as a place of history and heritage. This begs the following questions: What is a city? How do archaeologists define it, and how do they attempt to recreate the vibrancy of these places particularly in contexts where ancient cities and contemporary ones overlap?

Complexity: What Is a City?

Complexity studies have taken multiple forms with a legacy intimately connected to social-evolutionary frameworks seeking to measure "the number of parts in a system and number of interrelationships among those parts" (Sassaman 2004: 31; see also Alt 2010; Binford 1968; Earle 1987; Feinman and Neitzel 1984; Flannery 1972; Fried 1967; Renfrew et al. 1974; Service 1962; Wright 1984). These "parts" populated categories of trait lists derived from characteristics like the division of labor based on sex, accumulation of power, and the ability to control labor and redistribute goods archaeologically identified by the material representations of those traits that constitute a particular category of society (see Chapman 2003). This categorical system drew upon ethnographic examples comparing past societies with the contemporary where Western ideals of social organization constituted the "top of the evolutionary ladder" (Alt 2010: 2). The goal of such comparative studies was to create an expansive database of types of social organization, whereby each type was "concerned with macroscale processes and comparative studies that consider complex societies as monolithic and structured" (Baires 2017a: 55). And although this deterministic and comparative perspective has largely been abandoned, the idea of progressing from one complex social state to another still forms the basis of how archaeology theorizes past societies (see Chapman 2003; Pauketat 2007). Models of cross-cultural comparison focus on macroscale processes, which cannot truly address social variation; as Feinman (2012; see also Baires 2017a) states, such studies must consider the historical, cultural, and local factors that inform how societies form and act (see also Baires 2020; Pauketat 2013a). Categories of complexity provide limited frameworks of analysis because they consider the historically contingent factors that inform the long-term processes of social change. In the context of cities, histories (local, regional, and global) work to shape the formation of these urban environments through the integration and interaction of thousands of persons who come together in the creation of new and complex social relations. Cities are not ahistorical but places of origin "bringing together people, practices, and materials which simultaneously reference originating homelands" and create places anew (Baltus and Baires 2020: 124). This is social complexity.

Social complexity has shaped the discussion of societal types including the introduction of and focus on the archaeological city. The question – what is a city – is simple enough. Much archaeological research and theorizing have been devoted to this question (see Clark 2013; Smith 2010, 2014, 2020; Yoffee 2009, 2015; Yoffee and Terrentato 2015). Definitions have emerged based on lists of traits: a city is only a city if it includes a series of structures that govern social life. Similarly, cities were only identifiable if a set of particular sociopolitical thresholds were met: a ruler (or rulers) governed a large population that ascribed to a particular set of lifeways supported by a network of people who provided tribute, trade goods, and foodstuffs to the urban center (see Yoffee and Terrentato 2015). Archaeologically, cities were things of the Old World, not identified in pre-European-contact North America (until recently, of course [see Pauketat 2013a for a review]). North American societies (north of Mexico), from structural-functional perspectives, were never quite capable of moving beyond a "chiefdom": a hierarchically ordered community defined by its relative degree of social and political "complexity" (see Cobb 2003 for a review; see also Pauketat 2007). This conceptualization of Native North American societies as either a band, a tribe, or a chiefdom (à la Service 1962) contributed to how archaeological research framed the lifeways and social experiences of past Indigenous populations who were stuck in a social evolutionary loop that helped perpetuate the racialized undertones of the Moundbuilder Myth. I would argue that archaeological research never intended to become part of this legacy, but the discipline had a fraught connection to the study of Native American archaeological communities (see Deloria's 1992 commentary on this issue). The categorization of Native American societies into levels of complexity only fueled this fraught relationship. Each level marked an evolutionary transformation of a people, bringing them closer to the epitome of human social organization: Old World cities and states.

Today, the discipline has come to terms with this historical relationship and is moving well beyond it (see Alt 2010; Fowles 2013; Pauketat 2013b; Sassaman 2010), but its legacy remains in the ways archaeologists seek to classify the past, relinquishing it to a space devoid of human and other-than-human activity to focus on *structures* rather than *persons and processes*. Introducing a concept like the "city," then, to replace the previous categorizations of band, tribe, and chiefdom, must recognize this legacy and seek to move beyond it. How does the designation of a city, if applicable, aid in reframing the ways archaeologists think and theorize about the past? The city, if we follow the concepts laid out at the start of this section, should be engaged with as a dynamic force alive with the activity of multiple actors who ultimately shape and create the thing that then becomes "the city." The city, from this perspective, is alive just as much as the city inhabitants, *and* it defies temporal boundaries. I would advocate that archaeological studies of cities should be less concerned with structure and more concerned with how a city acts and how a city *feels* (see Yoffee 2015; see also Dan-Cohen 2017, 2020).

Norm Yoffee, in his 2015 edited volume on comparative cities, presented this idea of "catching the feel" of ancient cities based on the work of Moses Finley (1987) and Fustel de Coulanges (1864); both scholars looked to the ways a city was constructed by "actual people whose lives were structured by traditions and mentalities, but who also made decisions that led to social change" (Yoffee and Terrenato 2015: 10). For archaeologists, this idea of focusing on the people who populate a city rather than the structures that organize and create a city was novel. People, as agentic actors, were often left out of analyses of complex societies other than to note hierarchical organization based on the size of the city (see Wright and Johnson 1975, for example) or to focus on the ways cities navigate the redistribution of goods and demand tribute from its rural country-side (see Yoffee 2015; Yoffee and Terrenato 2015 for a summary; see also Smith 2014). This perspective on archaeological cities provides a static and sterile view of the past, the one that considers hierarchical, economic, and political structures as paramount to the experiential aspect of these places. Such perspectives are also more engaged with notions of social complexity than anything else, focusing on how a particular past community fits within the categorical models archaeologists create to understand the evolution of human social systems (see Alt 2010 for a review). This is particularly salient in North American archaeology where these models come with "very particular associations, possibilities, and constraints" (Alt 2010: 3) that bind the ways we think about the past.

If we return to Yoffee's call to "catch the feel" of cities, we must dispense with evolutionary models. First, we must recognize that cities are fusions of persons, places, landscapes, knowledge, and histories that shape the ways communities come together and create something new. Second, complexity is not something limited to a hierarchical social organization or even the evolutionary trajectory of those societal models, but rather is focused on how persons and processes of social life *were complex in and of themselves*. Complexity is entangled in and created by relationships: what persons did and how they shaped and practiced novel societal forms. Engaging with complexity in this way requires microscale analyses of the unique historical trajectories that shape and create complex social worlds (see Dan-Cohen 2020). This means that to see something as complex we must first begin with creating a fine-grained historical analysis of human and other-than-human social relationships.

This sort of meshwork analysis (à la Ingold 2012) considers how things relate to one another through growth and movement, which in a broader discussion of historical relationships is particularly useful. As we shall see, cities, and in particular the city of Cahokia, are never simple hierarchical structures but things that reach out and entwine themselves with other things, persons, and places. Each entwinement creates a novel experience or historical trajectory that all come together to shape the city. These experiences are accessible archaeologically in the material manifestations of those moments where things connect and create other things. This sort of microscale analysis examines the details of social life that then work to invent and build the story of the larger community.

So a city, if we are to attend to a definition, "provide[s] a phenomenology of experience, ranging from simple factors such as the streets available for pedestrian traffic to the most elaborate staged monuments and events" (Smith 2014: 317). Cities are palimpsests of landscape and experience that defy temporal boundaries creating places alive with the richness of social life. I will demonstrate that these things, moments, and persons are archaeologically accessible in the material culture and the human modification of spaces that make a city a city. Cities are built by persons; landscapes are shaped and transformed; and buildings, public plazas, walkways, farmlands, workshops, and neighborhoods are constructed and lived in. Daily life *is material*. The materiality of our world and daily life *makes* our life, making archaeology uniquely situated to access the experiences of past persons.

The Structure of the Element

The purpose of this Element is to analyze the processes of city creation and urbanization at the pre-Columbian North American city of Cahokia and to place it within the broader context of the Eastern Woodlands. While Cahokia was truly unique in terms of scale and experience, there is a legacy of community creation in the Eastern Woodlands providing the historical context for the emergence of Cahokia. This historical legacy is entangled with the knowledge and processes of mound building, the development of agricultural practices, the movement of persons over long distances, and the experiential aspects of the land entangled with historical memory. In the following, I focus on the processes of city-making at Cahokia by exploring the broader cultural context of the region as part of an assemblage of communities and histories rather than as an isolated phenomenon. The following sections focus on Cahokia's unique historical context, the histories of its precursors and contemporaries, as well as the ways Native American archaeological sites became part of the American historical narrative. I conclude by revisiting what makes Cahokia unique through a focus on what brought this place to life: the history of the landscape and the spiritual/religious aspects of the city's organizational layout that created a legacy of place, which remains a substantial aspect of our contemporary world.

2 Cahokia in Context

Cities are not unique Western phenomena; in fact, one of the oldest cities is Çatalhöyük, a Neolithic site located in present-day Turkey (see Hodder 2010: 456). This "embodied knowledge" is foundational to understanding how a city becomes a community and how a city maintains its community. Cities can be imaginaries – "places where futures are actively reimagined" through embodied experience derived from memory and space (Pauketat et al. 2015b: 456). The imagined aspect of a city is in its ability *to create and be created* and also in the notion that these complex places can emerge and reemerge again as products of newly imagined futures by those who inhabit and/or visit them (see Pauketat et al. 2015b; see Randall and Sassaman 2017). From a historical perspective, the emergence of the first city – Çatalhöyük – seemingly laid the groundwork for this imagination of urbanism ushering the global human population into the modern era; it brought to life the desire for a future that "provided socially inhabitable places," which were "in dialogue with ecology, tradition, place, person, and cosmos" (Randall and Sassaman 2017: 10). From this perspective, Cahokia can be understood as what Randall and Sassaman (2017: 10) conceptualize as a product of the middle ground – "a multi-temporal conceptual space, where cosmology, history and landscapes intersect" (see also Pauketat 2013b). Therefore, we must begin our examination of the city of Cahokia (occupied from AD 1050 to AD 1350) by looking first at the landscape of the American Bottom region of what is now southern Illinois in the United States of America to understand how the intersection of "ecology, tradition, place, person, and cosmos" (Pauketat 2013b) worked toward the creation of Native North America's first and only city north of the Rio Grande river. The remainder of this section highlights the natural and built landscapes with a keen focus on agriculture and the layout and construction of this early city.

Landscapes and Farming

The American Bottom is the rich floodplain landscape located where the Illinois, Missouri, and Mississippi Rivers meet. It extends from present-day

Alton, Illinois south to the town of Chester near the mouth of the Kaskaskia River and is composed of two major zones: the floodplain and the uplands each with their own distinct resources like rich, fertile soils for farming, oak-hickory forests, prairie grasslands, and accessible streams and creeks (see Baires 2017a; Betzenhauser 2011; Fowler 1997; Fritz 2019; Milner 1998; Pauketat 2013a; Welch 1975). Created by the movement of the Mississippi River over thousands of years, this landscape includes a series of abandoned river channels, oxbow lakes, marshes, swales, and tributary streams that absorb floodwaters (see Fowler 1997). The floodplain landscape of this region provided higher, sandier, and well-drained ridges ideal for cultivating crops, while the lower swales contained the clays often used in the construction of pottery and earthen mounds (see Baires 2017a for a review; see also Pauketat 2019). Important to note is the fact that this floodplain landscape, in addition to providing rich farmlands, was also a particularly swampy area. The ridge and swale landscape provided low points consistently filled in with floodwaters characteristic of a backswamp, river biome replete with muddy lowlands that amassed organic debris (see Milner 1998; see also Baires 2017a; Pauketat 2019). Some 19 percent of the floodplain immediately surrounding the city of Cahokia was covered by swamps and lakes with an additional 15 percent of the entire American Bottom region consistently inundated by water (Milner 1998: 45). Due to the clay subsoils in this region, most of the surface water did not adequately drain resulting in humid summer months and low areas of muddy pools and marsh vegetation that included resources like edible plants, water birds and fish, and mussel shells (Milner 1998: 44–49; see also Baires 2017a; Pauketat and Alt 2017). This combination of the floodplain ridges and swales resulted in an environment ripe with resources and, importantly, very amenable to farming, particularly in the Richland uplands to the south and east of Cahokia.

Corn, or maize (*Zea maize* L.), has often been seen as the premier agricultural crop of the Midwest and Cahokia (see Fritz 2019 for a summary) setting in motion the city's emergence and supporting its reign in the region as a large, regional polity. The argument typically went that maize appeared sometime in the Middle Woodland (300 BC–AD 400) period in the Midwest and slowly became intensified until it was the dominant agricultural crop in the region (see Emerson et al. 2020 for the summary; Fritz 2019; VanDerwarker et al. 2017). However, the dating of maize has changed recently (see Simon 2014, 2017), throwing out those early possibilities of maize appearing in the Middle Woodland and instead demonstrating that this crop did not become part of food and farming practices in the American Bottom region until after AD 900, or the late Terminal Late Woodland phase (AD 975–1050) (see Simon 2014; see also Emerson et al. 2020; Fritz 2019; Pauketat 2019). Prior to corn reaching the American Bottom, presumably brought through trade and/or by people migrating to the area, maize farming may have begun as early as the eighth century in the Arkansas River Valley at the Toltec site of the Plum Bayou culture (c. AD 700–1050) (Pauketat 2019). The presence of maize in the Arkansas River Valley was likely adopted from strains imported from the American Southwest and Northwest Mexico (Pauketat 2019; see also Rolingson 1998). These early farmers may have moved up from the Arkansas River Valley along with other Late Woodland groups like the Coles Creek culture from Arkansas, Mississippi, and Louisiana into the American Bottom bringing with them their knowledge of maize and how to grow it (Pauketat 2019; see also Alt 2019; Simon 2014, 2017). This knowledge of farming maize was likely accompanied by the knowledge of how to process it for consumption (e.g., nixtamalization) – both practices central to the development of this crop in the American Bottom by late Terminal Late Woodland peoples.

The introduction of maize in Illinois accompanied the farming system already in place – the one that included crops like sunflower, maygrass, erect knotweed, squash and other bottle gourds, and chenopod. Women tilled the fields, planted the seeds, and harvested the crops and, in fact, had done so since the beginnings of agriculture in the Eastern Woodlands. The practice of women farmers was documented by early European explorers and ethnographers, which provides the evidence to extrapolate that women were responsible for domesticating these crops as well (Fritz 2019; see also Hudson 1976). At contact, Native American men were described as not participating in nor holding the knowledge of farming and food practices, except when it came to the cultivation of the important and sacred crop of tobacco (Fritz 2019: 55). Fritz (2019) suggests that men grew this crop in small fields adjacent to their households and away from the fields where women grew staple foods. In addition to ethnographic evidence, iconography from the Cahokia area (red flint clay figurines depicting women in association with crops like sunflowers, gourds, and ancestor baskets (see Fritz 2019 for recent analysis) suggests that farming and the cultivation of crops were the spiritual domain of women who "contribute[d] to the well-being of their families and extended kin groups; they could enhance the status of selected segments of the community" by bringing agricultural goods to feasts and ceremonies, which may have "translated into political power" for some women (Fritz 2019: 47; see also Watson and Kennedy 1991) (Figure 4).

Importantly, these women farmers were well versed in the processes of how to plant and cultivate the starchy seed crops of the Eastern Agricultural Complex and already employed methods that could easily incorporate the planting of maize: predominantly the method of using digging sticks to create

Figure 4 Birger figurine, BBB motor site, Cahokia (photo by Tom Vickers, public domain, Wikimedia Commons)

holes for the sowing of corn kernels, a method already used in planting sunflower, for example. According to Fritz (2019: 70), corn would have been planted in fields directly in association with the crops of the Eastern Agricultural Complex, perhaps sown into sections or intercropped with squash plants whose vines may have climbed up the corn stalks. Maize was a welcomed crop and the one that added to the already complex agricultural system of farmers in the American Bottom.

With the introduction of maize to the diet, one can imagine that changes to lifeways would surely follow. Such changes are documented in the American Bottom at Terminal Late Woodland sites in southern Illinois, for one. Based on data from 25 communities containing 615 excavated structures and 3,400 pits, there is clear evidence for sedentary villages ranging in size from small farmsteads with 1–2 buildings to large villages with about 150 structures (Emerson et al. 2020; Fortier and McElrath 2002; Fritz 2019). Sometimes called the "Little Bang" (in juxtaposition to the "Big Bang" of Cahokia's emergence) in the American Bottom, this moment included the intensification of small village communities of households arranged in courtyards associated with large storage pits and, in some cases, ritual/special elite structures (e.g., the Range Site) (Brennan et al. 2018; Fortier and McElrath 2002; Fritz 2019; Kelly 1990, 2000). These changes increased population size and nucleation in the region through both in situ development and in-migration of people to the American Bottom (see Alt 2019; Emerson 2018; Hedman et al. 2018; Slater et al. 2014). The late Terminal Late Woodland (c. AD 975/1000) also introduced the process of nixtamalization: soaking kernels in a solution of water alkali, lime, and ash in stumpware pottery vessels to make hominy (Pauketat 2018; see also Benchley 2003). The use of nixtamalization by late Terminal Late Woodland peoples is further supported by the presence of large storage pits, presumably for surplus maize (Brennan et al. 2018), the use of large ceramic bowls perhaps for baking corn bread (Kelly 1980), and an increase in the presence of burned limestone, which may have been used to create the solution used in the nixtamalization of corn (McElrath et al. 2000; see also Emerson et al. 2020). For Cahokians, Pauketat (2019: 94) describes the impacts of the introduction of maize agriculture as being an assemblage of not just the crop itself but also *the practice* of nixtamalization. This practice entangled the growing and processing of corn with the knowledge of how to do it, the social networks needed to obtain the materials and the landscape itself. Limestone, a key component of nixtamalization, outcrops along the boundaries of the American Bottom floodplain, and Cahokian farmers would have had to alter their "everyday routines and relationships in order to acquire a steady supply of the rock and, as a consequence, complex supra- village networks of people-maize-limestone emerged," which worked, in part, to create Cahokia at AD 1050 (Pauketat 2019: 94).

One of Cahokia's founding practices included the extensive farming of the region. Its emergence as a city was entangled with the ability to farm large quantities of starchy seeds and maize, mostly in the Richland uplands, described as "the most likely engine that drove Cahokia's agricultural reorganization" (Benson et al. 2009; see also Alt 2019; Pauketat 2003). During Cahokia's emergence, c. AD 1050, this area benefited from a series of wet periods that provided the water necessary to grow large quantities of foodstuffs to feed a growing population of 10–15,000 people (Benson et al. 2009; Pauketat 2004). The Richland uplands (occupied from about AD 1000 to AD 1150 or Cahokia's peak [Pauketat 2003]), and the farmers who lived there, were essential to the emergence and sustainment of Cahokia – farming was a way of life that both developed out of the Terminal Late Woodland groups already occupying this space and by the regional immigrants who moved here to become part of whatever was happening at this ancient city (Alt 2019; see also Emerson 1997; Fritz 2019: 88–89; Pauketat 2013a). What is of particular interest regarding the Richland uplands is the diversity of this place. While the sites in the region (see Alt 2002, 2019 for an overview; see also Emerson and Hargrave 2000; Pauketat 2003) share some commonalities with Cahokia proper (in terms of house style, pottery, and other daily use items), there are important differences that manifest at the settlements excavated in the uplands. This includes specialized religious communities, small courtyard arrangements of houses, single-family farmsteads, at least one Cahokian religious/political outpost, and a community of nonlocal farmers with unique mortuary practices (see Alt 2019; see also Emerson 1997; Emerson and Hargrave 2000; Pauketat 2003). What these groups were doing in the Uplands is made clear by the artifact assemblages, somewhat dominated by stone hoes and re-sharpening flakes from re-sharpening hoes indicating a community emphasis on farming (see Alt 2019; Pauketat 2003). But importantly, these sites also demonstrate craft specialization, like the manufacture of fiber/twine (represented by the presence of spindle whorls), and the making of shell beads out of mollusk shells (see Alt 2019; Pauketat 2003). The Richland upland farmers were within a day's walk of "Downtown" Cahokia and express a unique focus on maintaining some of their original cultural traditions (seen in nonlocal pottery styles, for example) while also adopting "some of Cahokia's trappings" (Pauketat 2003: 55; see also Alt 2019). This interaction between the peoples of the Richland uplands and Cahokia indicates that the emergence and later dominance (culturally, religiously, and even politically) of this city were not based on an overt control of the region, but rather one that embraced pluralism whereby local and immigrant farmers "shaped the history of Cahokia" through participation in and adoption of Cahokian ways of life (Pauketat 2003: 58; see also Alt 2019). Cahokia and the historical processes of becoming part of this city (or Mississippianization) emphasize how the development and adoption of Cahokian practices, lifeways, and beliefs had been embraced beyond the city boundaries (see Pauketat 2002, 2004).

The City of Cahokia

The protected state site of Cahokia (the inner core of the city) was purchased by the state of Illinois and preserved in 1923. Prior to this purchase, an estimated half of this ancient city's mounds were destroyed due to the residential and commercial building projects of the late nineteenth and early twentieth centuries. When visiting the UNESCO World Heritage Site of Cahokia today, especially in the hot, humid summer months, the characteristics of this floodplain landscape come alive. Walking through this protected park, you experience the landscape as a living, breathing thing that uniquely situates the historical experiences of the Native American persons who created this place against a backdrop of modern urban sprawl. It can be difficult at times to separate yourself from this realm of modernity embodied in, for one, the two-lane highway that bisects the site, but if you visit Cahokia in the early morning or evening, the humidity, mists, and water-filled borrows and marshes created a visceral connection to the past, the one that emphasizes the power of this place and reminds us that water and watery places were of significant importance to Cahokians (Baires 2015, 2017a, 2017b; see also Pauketat 2019; Pauketat et al. 2017a).

The intersection of the American Bottom landscape and the built environment of Cahokia create an urban space composed of earthen monuments, plazas, causeways, households, and neighborhoods entangled with streams, oxbow lakes, creeks, prairie grasslands, forests, and the nearby limestone bluffs. The city of Cahokia, some 20 km^2, consisted of three precincts (St. Louis, East St. Louis, and Cahokia) and an estimated 200 mounds that cross the Mississippi River from present-day Collinsville, Illinois, to St. Louis, Missouri (see Figure 2), rapidly coalescing "around a political leader, a religious movement, or a kin-coalition" that centralized politics and social relations (Pauketat 2002: 152). This "Big Bang," as Pauketat (1994) describes it, draws upon archaeological research from multiple excavations of different Cahokian neighborhoods (Tract 15A, Dunham Tract, ICT-II, Grand Plaza, Mound 72, FAI-270) revealing, c AD 1050, a rapid transformation of the immediate American Bottom landscape. This included the abandonment of some of the Terminal Late Woodland lifeways previously discussed for the adoption of a Cahokia-specific plan: wall-trench, semisubterranean style houses, a grid orientation of those houses and neighborhoods to a 5° offset alignment, the construction of earthen mounds, and the central Grand Plaza not to mention the addition and expansion of the farmlands in the Richland uplands. This process of urbanization included the drastic reorientation of the landscape, immigration, and in situ transitions of local populations who adopted these new Cahokian lifeways (Alt 2010, 2019). This means that those Terminal Late Woodland peoples already residing in the American Bottom embraced this new Cahokian way of life; this transformation brought at least an additional estimated 15,000 people to the region through processes of immigration (Pauketat 2002; Pauketat and Lopinot 1997; Slater et al. 2014). Persons came from southeastern Missouri, northeastern and east-central Arkansas, and the Yankeetown region of southern Indiana and northern Kentucky (Alt 2019; Pauketat 2009; see also Fritz 2019: 89). Cahokia became a place of new and old traditions cradled in the floodplain landscape.

Water is a prominent fixture in the American Bottom floodplain that takes many forms at Cahokia (Figure 5). In this region, rainfall can vary between 58

Figure 5 Mounds 61 and 62, water-filled borrow pit (photo by the author)

and 175 cm in a single year, which also contributes to this slow drainage creating muddy bottomlands. The nineteenth-century explorer and scholar, Henry Brackenridge, toured the American Bottom region near Cahokia recording his observations along Cahokia Creek – a small tributary of the Mississippi River describing the landscape as wetland prairie full of swampy features buffeted by limestone bluffs (see Baires 2015). Similarly, Charles Dickens (1987[1842]: 220–221) portrayed this landscape as one of the stagnant floodwaters and an "unbroken slough of black mud and water . . . [with] no variety but in depth." These explorers paint a picture of Cahokia that recalls uninhabitable muddy lands with sluggish waterways unsuitable for housing the largest city in North America, north of Mexico. But contrary to these nineteenth-century observations, *it was*, in part, the mud and water that made Cahokia suitable and desirable to the thousands of Native American persons who resided there. Water is life, and the excessive presence of it at Cahokia (especially during its emergence at AD 1050, due to frequent rainfall [Benson et al. 2009]) not only created farmable lands but also facilitated more ephemeral connections between the living world and the world of the ancestors (see Baires 2017a, 2017b).

Within the 5 m^2 that the Cahokia precinct immediately occupies, 100 ha of land had the potential to be inundated by water during the wettest months of the year (see Munoz et al. 2014, 2015; see also Milner 1998). When combined with elevations obtained from LiDAR topography maps (125.7–126.4 m asl), areas at risk for flooding or areas with a regular presence of low levels of water include two ridge-top mortuary mounds (Mound 72 and Rattlesnake Mound) and the central Rattlesnake Causeway (Baires 2017a) located along the center-line of the Cahokia precinct. In contrast, Monks Mounds, the Grand Plaza, and Mounds 42 and 41 along with several densely populated neighborhoods are in areas that range between 127 and 128 m asl, or 1–2 m above elevations at risk for flooding (see Baires 2015 for a summary). What does this mean? Cahokian builders recognized the power of water and the role it played in their landscape; they built neighborhoods, platform mounds, and the Grand Plaza at elevations above flood levels by building up and intentionally filling in and flattening out the ridge and swale topography. This technique was used to construct the Grand Plaza (c. 19–24 ha in size), which created a large, flat, and well-drained public space (Dalan et al. 2003). In juxtaposition to the Grand Plaza, the kilometer-long earthen causeway (Baires 2017a) that connects Cahokia's central precinct (beginning out the southern edge of the Grand Plaza) to the city's southern boundary was built through the city's backswamp, muddy landscape ending at the prominent burial mound – Rattlesnake Mound. This raised earthen cause-way was built as a foundational piece to this city and intentionally constructed in a wet, murky bottomland orienting Cahokia's organizational layout to a 5° offset orthogonal design (more on this later) (Baires 2017a; see also Pauketat 2013; Pauketat et al. 2015b; Romain 2015a). Here we can glimpse the vision Cahokia's builders had – to create a connection between the living world (as embodied in Monks Mound and other similarly elevated locations) and the realm of the ancestors personified by the watery, murky landscape south of the city's Downtown core (see Baires 2015, 2017a).

This swampy landscape was tapped for two important aspects of Cahokian lifeways: mound-building materials and the clays to make early Mississippian pottery (see Baires 2017a; Brennan et al. 2018; Pauketat 2018; Pauketat and Alt 2017). When you mix this clay with crushed and burned mussel shells, you get prime material to make low-fired pots for cooking, storage, and religious/ritual purposes. As Pauketat describes, "the watery relations linking people and other-than-human powers were also assembled in the hands of people via the manu-facture of the city's pottery wares" where "the production of cooking jars made from backswamp clays at the beginning of the urban- construction phase of Greater Cahokia around AD 1050 was restricted to certain times and certain people" (2019: 94). Similarly, sod blocks of the black, soggy clays used to make Cahokian pottery wares also served as the building blocks of the mounds of Cahokia (see, e.g., Schilling 2012). These clays were dug from the marshy landscapes creating large, open pits (called borrows, alluding to the borrowing of sediments for construction materials) that either remained waterlogged locations or were sometimes intentionally filled in in the same manner used to build the mounds (Baires and Baltus 2019). Basket loads of these clays, sod blocks, and lenses of sandier soils created the layers of Cahokia's mounds embedding the natural world and its waters into the city infrastructure. Mounds took the shape of rectangular and circular platforms and ridgetops, the former typically housing a rectangular or circular structure and/or marker post (on the summit of Monks Mound, there was a very large ritual/political building and a marker post) and the latter serving as places for the burial of human and other-than-human persons (see Baires 2017a, 2017b for a summary) (Figure 6). The sourcing of clay for mound building and pottery suggests that the knowledge and practice of how to create the city of Cahokia were literally buried in the land, sustained by the connection among persons (mud, water, soil, and human), which resulted in the creation of their world.

This world was further shaped by the pole-and-thatch structures built in neighborhoods, on mounds and platforms, and along the edges of borrow pits and other watery locales where Cahokia's subcommunities "provide insight into the relationships between Cahokian space and changing notions of neighborhood, community, and cosmos" (Betzenhauser and Pauketat 2019: 137). With the emergence of Cahokia (Lohmann phase, AD 1050) as a planned city, those Terminal Late Woodland courtyard groups and small villages were supplanted by Cahokian-style wall-trench houses, steam baths, and large square buildings aligned to a site-wide grid set up by the Rattlesnake Causeway (Baires 2017a; Betzenhauser and Pauketat 2019). Neighborhoods from three areas of Cahokia document the association of residential homes with religious buildings, like medicine lodges, which housed sacred bundles in alcoves (Collins 1990; Pauketat 1994, 1998; see also Betzenhauser and Pauketat 2019). The adherence to this strict grid was all but abandoned by the end of the Stirling phase (AD 1200), when a large bastioned palisade went up around the central core of the site and other residential areas were replaced by Woodhenge (c. AD 1100; a celestial clock of sorts) and other ritual/religious structures (Betzenhauser and Pauketat 2019). The Moorehead phase (post AD 1250) at Cahokia saw almost a complete abandonment of any of the prescribed order of the city's first 150 years – neighborhoods were abandoned and largely constricted (see Baltus 2014). Changes to Cahokia's domestic order reflect a move away from the strict imposition of order emplaced at Cahokia's emergence to a breakdown of that order derived from a shifting notion of what it meant to be part of the Cahokian community (see Betzenhauser and Pauketat 2019).

Figure 6 Downtown Cahokia, Monks Mound in the background (Michael Hampshire, permissions granted from Cahokia Mounds State Museum)

In addition to domestic houses and large, ritual/religious and political build-ings, Pauketat (2019: 94; see also Alt 2019; Pauketat et al. 2017a) has argued that Cahokia's wet areas were marked by circular rotundas and steam baths – or as he calls them "water shrines" ranging in size from 5 to 500 m². These structures, often built atop circular platforms, overlooked "seeps or bodies of water both at Cahokia's outlying Emerald Acropolis and at its St. Louis pre-cinct" further indicating the importance of water to Cahokia's infrastructure (Pauketat 2019: 95). Cahokia's landscape also included large square council houses (or temples), T- and L-shaped buildings, small rectangular domiciles, and large free-standing posts (Alt 2019; Betzenhauser and Pauketat 2019; Emerson 1997; Pauketat 2013a; Skousen 2012a). These posts were large (oftentimes 10 m tall, 1 m diameter), cypress logs floated upriver from "cypress-swamp forests in southern Illinois and Missouri, where they grow today" (Pauketat 2019: 96; see Lopinot 1992).

Large logs of red cedar were used in the creation of Cahokia's Woodhenge – an imposing solstitial calendar that tracked the solstices and the equinoxes by marking the sunrise using a center observation post. The posts were erected in a series of five circles over a period from AD 900 to AD 1100 ranging in size from 12 to 60 posts. The use of red cedar and the presence of a red pigment in postholes suggest that these large, upright posts were painted. Red cedar is often considered a sacred wood that grows well in the dry soils common on the bluff tops of southwestern Illinois (see Simon 2002; see also Pauketat 2002). Woodhenge was likely used to mark not only the solstices and equinoxes but also agriculture festivals and the changing seasons creating a calendar for the city's inhabitants (Iseminger 2010; Wittry 1969).

In addition to marking the movement of the sun, Cahokian builders also marked the movement of the moon (see Alt 2019; Pauketat 2013a, 2017; Pauketat et al. 2015b; Romain 2015a, 2017; see also Baires 2015, 2017a). A bit more ephemeral in its movement through the night sky than the sun through the day, the moon was a powerful celestial body with a unique cycle, which takes 18.6 years to complete, due to its orbit around the earth at an angle five degrees off the earth's own ecliptic (Pauketat 2017: 4). This cycle can be observed on earth as "extreme rising and setting positions of the full moon" where the moon rises and sets at its maximum positions to the north and south of the summer and winter solstices and then again rises and sets 9.3 years later "at minimum positions inside the envelope formed by the solstices" (Pauketat 2013a, 2017: 4; Romain 2015a, 2017). This complex lunar cycle was part of a historical knowledge of the cosmos that dates at least to the Middle Woodland (150 BCE–400 AD), but perhaps also to the 3,500-year-old Late Archaic site of Poverty Point located in present-day Louisiana (see Brecher and Haag 1983;

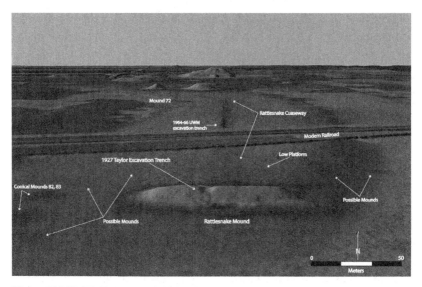

Figure 7 LiDAR Downtown Cahokia and the Rattlesnake Causeway (LiDAR data courtesy the Illinois State Archaeological Survey; image by the author [Baires 2017a])

Hively and Horn 2013; Lepper 2004, 2006; Romain 2000; see also Pauketat 2017; Sassaman 2005). It is this history of sky watching, and more particularly moon watching, that was built into the emergence of Cahokia. The construction of the Rattlesnake Causeway c. AD 1050, for one, orders the city grid to the moon's 18.6-year cycle and "served as the baseline for Cahokia's 5° offset city grid" (Pauketat 2017: 13; see also Baires 2017a; Pauketat 2013a; Pauketat et al. 2015b; Romain 2015a). This causeway also connected Monks Mound, the plaza, and residential neighborhoods to the murky swamps and mortuary mounds on the city's southern edge (Baires 2017a; Figure 7).

Cahokia's lunar-aligned cosmic ordering sits in juxtaposition to the solstitial calendar of Woodhenge, where both sets of alignments work to assemble the city itself. And once more, these alignments are not limited to the Cahokia precinct alone but manifest in the peripheral communities of the Emerald Acropolis in the Richland uplands and Trempealeau Mounds, a Cahokian outpost in Wisconsin (Pauketat 2013a; Pauketat et al. 2017a; Boszhardt et al. 2015).

East St. Louis and St. Louis

Discussions of the city of Cahokia would be remiss without the addition of the archaeological sites of East St. Louis and St. Louis (see Figure 2). These sites, located immediately to the southwest of Cahokia and spanning across a 10-km-long area of oxbow lakes, Cahokia Creek, and the Mississippi River, are superimposed, today, by the urban sprawl of St. Louis, Missouri. Between c. AD 1100 and AD 1200, Cahokia, East St. Louis, and St. Louis coexisted and created a regional complex of earthen mounds, pole-and-thatch structures, and networks of relationships including a shared political and religious structure that emphasized the entanglement of the cosmos with the built environment as embodied in and through mounds, causeways, and neighborhoods. Together, these three precincts housed almost 200 earthen mounds, with Cahokia and East St. Louis being the largest of the three. Not much is known about the St. Louis precinct; it was destroyed in the nineteenth century leaving behind little information (see Betzenhauser and Pauketat 2019). We do know that like Cahokia and East St. Louis, the St. Louis Mound Group was composed of a planned layout of twenty-six earthen mounds that included platforms and ridgetops – in fact, one of its largest mounds was the ridgetop burial mound Big Mound (Byers 2006; Kelly 1994; Pauketat 2004). Like the St. Louis Mound group, East St. Louis and Cahokia were both impacted by early urban sprawl during the nineteenth and twentieth centuries: East St. Louis's mounds were removed in the late 1800s, and an estimated half of Cahokia's mounds were removed around the same time (see Betzenhauser and Pauketat 2019 for a summary).

Much of the information we have on the East St. Louis Mound (ESTL) group stems from recent large-scale excavations conducted by the Illinois State Archaeological Survey from 2008 to 2012. This project was conducted in advance of the construction of the New Mississippi River Bridge and revealed over 6,000 precontact archaeological features. The data obtained is immense and provides a new lens to examine Cahokia's spread and impact across the American Bottom floodplain. East St. Louis appears to be a unique component of the city of Cahokia: one that was relatively short-lived (AD 1050–1250) yet left an impact on the region. The layout of East St. Louis included an estimated forty-five mounds organized in semicircular fashion as well as public spaces with large, upright posts, temple buildings, storage huts, and walled compounds (Brennan 2021; Fortier 2007; Pauketat 2004, 2005; Pauketat et al. 2015b). Orientations of buildings at ESTL fluctuated from the Lohmann to Stirling phases. After AD 1050, ESTL buildings were oriented to a precinct-wide axis of 75 degrees of azimuth (Betzenhauser and Pauketat 2019; Brennan et al. 2018). Later, in the Stirling phase, buildings shifted their orientation to the cardinal directions and a grid-like pattern that seems to reference the historically recorded locations of the mounds once there. The households that remained in the Moorehead phase (like those Downtown Cahokia) were orientated to small community clusters, rather than any site-wide grid or plan (Betzenhauser and Pauketat 2019).

At the onset of the Lohmann phase, small pre-Mississippian villages of no more than 400 people increased to at least 5,000 and over the life span of ESTL neighborhoods transformed to incorporate a rigid organizational grid like the Cahokia precinct (Brennan et al. 2018; see Betzenhauser and Pauketat 2019). The site alignments recorded at East St. Louis indicate that this precinct, like Cahokia, adhered to some kind of "rigidity of order" that would have "restrained, enabled, and patterned the movements of residents and visitors" (Betzenhauser and Pauketat 2019: 141). But, unlike Cahokia, strict domestic neighborhoods are few and far between; instead, Cahokia's "architecture of power" (see Emerson 1997) that includes large rectangular and circular structures, T- and L-shaped buildings, and marker posts is interspersed with domestic houses. For example, in some areas, houses "of one kind or another were built directly over the remnant post pit locations" once these posts were decommissioned and removed at around AD 1100 (Betzenhauser and Pauketat 2019: 138; see also Skousen 2012a, 2012b). Then, in the Stirling phase (AD 1100), ESTL expanded southward in a preplanned grid arrangement consisting of large square structures interspersed with steam baths, storage structures, and large rectangular houses. This arrangement consisted of both domestic debris and highly specialized architecture leading Betzenhauser and Pauketat (2019; see also Brennan et al. 2018) to conclude that this area was home to elite families. By the Moorehead phase, ESTL activity dwindled, and the precinct was almost completely abandoned, except for the construction of platform mounds and the burial of mortuary remains; one residential courtyard group was left – perhaps to oversee these last vestiges of community life at ESTL (Betzenhauser and Pauketat 2019; Brennan et al. 2018). It is clear from recent excavations at ESTL that its relationship to the Cahokia precinct was, in some ways, about bringing people (human and otherwise) together in buildings and through built landscapes that emphasized the ordered relationships of the persons who inhabited these spaces.

The City Imagined

In this section, I examined how the city of Cahokia was built upon and entangled with the natural landscape of the region as well as the historical connections to knowledge of the place. This knowledge of the place reminds us that the land is the "designator of how living beings will organize," and it works to create social worlds that bring together multiple agentic persons (Watts 2013b: 23). From this perspective, the land is the foundation for a city's growth and change, *and* it holds the histories and knowledge required to construct such a city. To examine archaeological cities means we must place them within the broader historical context to consider how knowledge of the place may inform and contextualize their construction. To build a city is a part of our shared global humanity. Cities are not an isolated phenomenon of modernity but places representing a new social order in which multiple groups must coexist (Smith 2010; see also De Munck 2017). This is the truly amazing part about a city – the fact that thousands of diverse persons come together to create something shared.

Cities and urban centers may come into existence for various reasons, which may include ceremony and religion, politics and economics, and/or trade and exchange. But, as Smith states, "the key to the success of cities must lie in their social aspects" where community relations and kinship ties are reified and where "social contacts are diversified, and neighborhoods become the principal geographic anchor of social interaction" (2010: 3–4). In the case of Cahokia, social relations among persons were embodied in and through the modification and incorporation of the natural environment for the construction of earthen mounds, plaza spaces, causeways, farmland, and neighborhoods. The construction of the city's three precincts of Cahokia, East St. Louis, and St. Louis created a network of persons connected through mounds and architectural features that spread out across the American Bottom floodplain. The Cahokian landscape was intentional. The orientation of buildings, mounds, neighborhoods, and plazas align with the ideologies of the persons who built them. These ideologies were experienced through the farming of crops and their ties to the women farmers who held that traditional knowledge (see Fritz 2019). They were alive in the positioning of the Cahokia precinct through the Rattlesnake Causeway to the moon and the cosmos (see Baires 2017a; Pauketat 2013a). This ever-present Cahokia order (AD 1050–1250) constructed social life and was compelling enough to bring thousands of people to the American Bottom floodplain to participate in it. In the next section, I discuss the broader medieval Mississippian world to examine Cahokia's reach and influence beyond the American Bottom while also considering the historical context of the emergence of Cahokia as a place.

3 The Global Mississippian World and Its Forebearers

Cahokia did not emerge in a vacuum; its presence is preceded by the Moundbuilders who left their mark across the Eastern Woodlands beginning some time ago, c. 5000 BCE. This "mark" included the practice of building traditions and communities along with the mounds themselves. Communities in this context are not limited to one particular historical moment or geographic locale, nor are they composed solely of human beings. These communities include a variety of entities, from celestial bodies to the soil used to build the mounds; communities are both physical and citational places with participants distributed across vast geographic areas and temporalities (see Section 2; see Pauketat and Sassaman 2020; see Baltus and Baires 2020; Brennan 2021). At this statement, you might be thinking that this is much too broad of a way to conceptualize the past of Moundbuilders – communities need boundaries of geography, time, place, and persons to exist. Boundaries provide a sense of knowable limits and thus create the said community. But if we were to suspend that reality for a moment, we may see that the communities reviewed in this section were constituted not by boundaries of place alone. Instead, these communities were "global" (global here refers to the then-known world of Moundbuilders, the Eastern Woodlands; Wright 2017, 2020; see also Baires 2020; Henry and Miller 2020) and based on a shared ontological understanding of the world within which they lived (see Pauketat and Sassaman 2020: 311). This shared ontological understanding might be akin to what Western societies think of as religion, but in the context of the mound-building Eastern Woodlands, religion is animistic (see Pauketat 2013a for a review). This means a person's world is created by the relationships among any agentic being (e.g., the soils used to build mounds, celestial bodies, human beings, spirits, etc.). There is no division between the spiritual and physical worlds, no divide between the subject and the object (see Descola 2013; Hornborg 2006; Ingold 2000; see also Alberti and Marshall 2009; Todd 2016; Watts 2013b). The animistic world is one of participation, whereby "individuals actively engage nonhuman agents in the course of everyday practice" (Pauketat and Sassaman 2020: 275).

This animist worldview and a focus on the relational qualities of social life inform the historical context of mound building in the Eastern Woodlands. As discussed in Section 1, history (from an animist/relational perspective) is not linear and is not simply "of the past," but rather part of the present and the future. Time is cyclical. In this sense, building histories and building communities share a commonality in that both rely upon relationships among multiple persons (not all of whom are human), places, and experiences (see Watts Malouchos 2021 for a review). This means that mounds as palimpsests of earth, beings, and time persist to create new futures through their continued existence and participation in the present "where cosmology, history, and landscape intersect" (Randall and Sassaman 2017: 10). Furthermore, modifying the landscape (through mound building, for example) creates a space to revisit and "resocialize" previously inhabited spaces, bringing that space (and its attendant traditions) back into the present (see Ingold 2012; Randall and Sassaman 2017).

In the Eastern Woodlands of Native North America, these traditions began in the Middle Archaic period broadly encompassing societies that built mounds of earth to groups who erected shell rings along coastal and river waters in the southeastern parts of North America. These traditions persisted into the Woodland period with the Adena and Hopewell societies of the Midwest and Midsouth, followed by the Mississippian traditions of mound building that permeated the Eastern Woodlands from the Great Lakes to the Gulf of Mexico and from the Mississippi River to the Appalachian Mountains (see Figure 1; see Kassabaum 2019 for a general review). The mounds and mound-building practices of the Eastern Woodlands encompass a broad range of mound types, styles, methods of construction, mound uses, and associated materials. In this section, I review select examples from each time period to provide context for the emergence of Cahokia and a foundation to explore the impact this great city had on the region. This review is in no way exhaustive but instead focuses on prime examples of the manipulation of the earth in the Eastern Woodlands for the creation of new communities.

Middle to Late Archaic c. 5000 BCE–1000 BCE

The southeast records the earliest instances of mound building by early hunter-gatherers beginning about 5000 BCE. Constructed of earth and shell, Archaic mounds likely marked the abandonment of a settlement with a "capping" event and were used as cemeteries or as isolated monuments not tied to a particular settlement or cemetery. The earliest iterations of Archaic mounds date between 5,700 and 4,700 years constructed in stages resulting in a final conical shape. No known mound-top buildings at these early sites have been documented, but some conical mounds have pre-mound structures (Kuttruff 1997; Saunders 1994; see Topping 2010). Perhaps one of the most well-documented and largest Middle Archaic mound sites is Watson Brake (located in Louisiana, dates to c. 3350 BC–3000 BC) with 11 mounds connected by low ridges and arranged in an oval shape (Saunders et al. 2005). This small mound complex was likely a place of permanent residence, with subsistence evidence (vertebral faunal assemblage dominated by fish) supporting a year-round occupation (Saunders et al. 2005). Fire-cracked rock, lithics and lithic debitage, baked clay objects, and evidence for making stone beads are also documented in the residential and workshop areas at Watson Brake (Saunders et al. 2005). While the artifacts accumulated for this site are dense, indicating a year-round occupation, questions remain as to why Watson Brake was constructed and ultimately what its purpose was.

Joe Saunders (2004) largely argues that this place was not built to be used solely as an economic center nor simply for extra-regional gathering, but instead (following Clark 2004) suggests that Watson Brake (like so many other mound complexes) was constructed for ceremonial reasons. This complex, along with two other Middle Archaic mound sites (Caney and Frenchman's Bend), share practices of design that may be indicative of "a regional-scale moundscape ... [where] alignments may point to pathways or circuits of movement among complexes" (Pauketat and Sassaman 2020: 346; see Clark 2004; Saunders 2010). When thinking of the broader history of Native American places in the Eastern Woodlands, Watson Brake (and its contemporaries) suggests that the ideas and knowledge associated with mound building "circulated freely" embodied in the design, erection, and experiential aspects of these mound site complexes (Saunders et al. 2005: 664). Meaning, as these sites persisted on the land (during occupation and post-abandonment), they informed and impacted those persons who lived among them, traveled by them, and told the stories of their existence.

Like the mound complexes of the Middle Archaic located in Louisiana, the shell rings and mounds of the coastal and riverine Southeast date between 8,500 and 3,000 years cal BP. These shell rings and mounds coincide with the beginnings of pottery manufacture and a drop in sea-level rise providing lucrative estuarine environments stable enough to support coastal living. In general, the shape and size of these monuments vary with few U-shaped rings up to 300 m in length and others as wide as 100 m and enclosed. Shell mounds, on the other hand, can rise to 12 m in height. Ring and mound construction consist of shells, earth, bone, and artifacts. Unlike their earthen counterparts of the Middle Archaic, the stratigraphic layers of shell rings and mounds vary widely and may demonstrate evidence of living surfaces as well as large-scale feasting events evidenced by massive deposits of shells (Marquardt 2010; Russo and Heide 2001; Sanger et al. 2020; Sassaman 2006; Saunders 2004, 2017; Saunders and Russo 2011). Centers of mounded rings were usually "clean" plaza spaces, however, at the St. Catherine's shell ring in Georgia large pits were in the ring's center (Sanger and Thomas 2010). Other variations include the presence of cremation in association with copper at the center of the McQueen Ring (Sanger 2015). Shell mounds were heaping piles of shell and earth accumulated over long periods of time with extensive evidence for both habitation and human burials – created as people came back generation after generation (Moore and Thompson 2012; Pauketat and Sassaman 2020: 242).

The mounds of the Shell Mound Archaic (SMA) range in size with the largest areas covering up to 24,281 m^2 with mound heights upward of 12 m. These mounds accrued over thousands of years in some cases and consist of complex stratigraphy of whole or crushed shells and feature deposits like fire pits, hearth dumps, and fired clay floors (see Saunders 2017 for a detailed summary). Stratigraphic layers from SMA mounds do contain evidence of daily living, but it is likely that these habitations were seasonal and perhaps abandoned during spring floods (Pauketat and Sassaman 2020). Of particular interest here is the presence of burials – some estimate 18,000 (Claassen 2010) – located in these shell mounds. So many burials were present, in fact, that Cheryl Claassen (2010) argues that the primary purpose of these places was to bury the dead. The association of shells to dead bodies is of particular importance as these connections are intimately entangled with notions of renewal and rebirth and the cyclical nature of life (Claassen 2010, 2011). Shell is something sourced from the water, which has connections to the primordial waters of world origin (see Claassen 2011; see also Baires 2017a, 2017b). For the burials of the SMA associated with shell, bodies seem to be interred in a variety of ways either in, under, or beside shell deposits with or without associated artifacts and in flexed or extended positions. Evidence also suggests some dead suffered violent deaths and, in the case of burials from Green River, may indicate conflict among groups (Claassen 2010; see also Marquardt and Watson 2005; Pauketat and Sassaman 2020).

Related to the mound sites of the SMA in the Midsouth is Stallings Island (mid-Savannah River region) considered to be a cultural center of the region as well as a mortuary area occupied during at least two distinctive habitation sequences (between 5,000 and 3,200 cal BP; Sassaman et al. 2006). Stallings Island also boasts some of the oldest pottery in North America. During the "Classic Stalling's" occupation (marked by the use of a specific type of decorated pottery, which includes the carinated bowl) people likely held feasts associated with mortuary rituals drawing people into the community at certain parts of the year (Sassaman 2006; Saunders 2017). Sassaman et al. (2006: 561) argue that Stallings Island with its combined "changes in technology, such as the addition of pottery in general, as well as the lesser-known innovations, such as the use of pit storage, carinated bowls, and specialized antler points" reflects the "cost of intensified ritual activity" making these places persistent on the landscape (à la Thompson 2010).

The St. Johns River shell mounds (c. 7300 cal BP, located in peninsular Florida) served their communities as "persistent places" as well with evidence of activity continuing well into the Woodland and Mississippian periods (Sassaman and Randall 2012; Saunders 2017). These shell mounds were part of settlements that included "linear or crescent-shaped shell ridges; platform mounds created with intermittent lenses of clean shell, burned shell and sand; shell and sand mortuary structures; and conical burial mounds of sand and shell" (Saunders 2017: 11). As Randall notes (2013), the most numerous site types of the St. Johns River Valley shell mounds are ridges, which range in size from 45 to 200 m in length and between 2.0 and 8.3 m in height. Seasonally occupied, these ridges were likely domestic sites, while their multi-mound complex counterparts (much larger in size 300–600 m in volume and more than 10 m high) were often utilized after the close of the Archaic (see Randall 2013). In addition, shell and sand mortuary mounds were an important feature of this landscape constructed over extended periods of time; burials were placed within deposits of shell and white or brown sand (Randall 2013). According to Randall (2013: 214), the peoples of the St. John's River Valley shell mounds and ridges "were concerned with their own history" as evidenced by the continuous coming back to and replacing previous habitations with ceremonial spaces like burial mounds and platforms (see Randall 2013: 214).

Until recently (see Saunders 2017 for a review), shell rings and mounds were thought to be the trash mounds resulting from the harvesting of shells for consumption. But this benign take ignores information, specifically regarding the importance of shells as agentic beings and the significance of the use of landscape as a mechanism for conveying histories (see Claassen 2010; see also Baires 2017a; Sassaman and Randall 2012). Throughout the Eastern Woodlands, shell and shell objects are tied to "rebirth and rejuvenation" (Claassen 2010: 173), documented in burial mounds and other mortuary contexts (see also Sassaman 2006). Shell (according to Matt Sanger [2015]) "carried a heavy symbolic load" (Saunders 2017: 3). The symbolic significance of shell remained in its ability to create social ties and bring people together through "purposeful act[s], replete with social meaning" (Claassen 2010; Saunders 2017). Shell rings and mounds became "centers for population aggregation, ceremony, and feasting" (Saunders 2017: 22) where monumentality can be explained as "a medium of discursive practice that structures the trajectory and pace of culture change" in the region (Sassaman and Randall 2012: 55). The mounds and rings of the Middle Archaic present us with an enticing view of past historical practice that emphasizes how persons navigate their ties to place as "historical resources" (Sassaman and Randall 2012: 57). The tradition of mound building begins here in the Eastern Woodlands evidenced by the monumental-building projects that populate the landscape and by the consistent visitation to and reuse of these places. Shell mounds and rings lived their own life histories built on the knowledge accumulated over generations and in some ways laid the groundwork (literally) for the emergence of other Archaic mound sites – in particular Poverty Point, perhaps the most well-known Late Archaic mound community located in northeast Louisiana (1600–1200 BCE), that came after.

Discussions of the historical significance of mound building in the Eastern Woodlands must include Poverty Point, perhaps one of the most important mound sites in North America. Theories about the purpose of Poverty Point populate the imagination of archaeologists and descriptions range from a seasonal meeting place to a thriving proto-city (see Gibson 2001; Sassaman 2005; Spivey et al. 2015). The site is massive covering an area of over 3 km^2 in the Macon Ridge area of northeast Louisiana and situated above a bayou where the Mississippi and Arkansas Rivers once flowed.

Poverty Point boasts six concentric earthen ridges that form one half of a circle that established a large and central plaza space about 600 m wide. This plaza space and the ridges that enclose it open to the east and Bayou Macon. The ridges are crossed by four aisles breaking them up into six sections. In between each ridge is a swale, perhaps where soils were taken to build up the ridges. Archaeological excavations revealed the presence of postholes, hearths, and middens under and on the ridges indicative of habitation. Six additional mounds complete the Poverty Point complex. They are aligned on north/south axes to the west of the concentric ridges and to the east. Mounds A, B, and E constitute one north/south alignment located just to the west of the rings. Mound A is the largest mound shaped like a bird flying west (Figure 8). Mound B (located 600 m to the north of Mound A) is dome-shaped, while Mound E (183 m to the south) is flat-topped and referred to as Ballcourt Mound. Mound C and Motley Mound compose a second north/south axis about 600 m east of the first. Motley Mound may also represent a bird flying to the north. Mound D is located just east of the southern and interior-most ridge and was built some 2,000 years after Poverty Point's abandonment (Gibson 2001, 2007; Kidder 2002; Sassaman 2005; see also Pauketat and Sassaman 2020).

Jon Gibson (2001) argues that the inner ring of the concentric ridges was built first while the remaining ridges followed from inside out. After the construction of the ridges came the mounds: Mound B was built first, followed by Mounds E, C, and A and Motley Mound (Ortmann 2010; Ortmann and Kidder 2012 see also Sherwood and Kidder 2011. According to Ortmann, "virtually all earth-work construction at Poverty Point appears to have taken place during the approximately 800-year timeframe that constitutes the terminal end of the Late Archaic in the Lower Mississippi River Valley" (2010: 675). And further-more, each of these mounds was constructed rapidly. For example, it is very likely that Mound A was built in as little as three months suggesting an organized labor force adhering to a planned design (Ortmann 2010; Ortmann and Kidder 2012). As Sassaman describes it "the construction of Poverty Point

Figure 8 Poverty Point Mound A (image by the author)

indeed was eventful," but this construction was only part of the story including the "materialization or interpretation of ancient experiences, *the invention of tradition*" (2005: 336, emphasis added). This "invention of tradition" is the product of multiple histories converging in one locale whereby Poverty Point becomes a cosmopolitan place (Sassaman 2005). Not only are peoples from disparate parts of the Upper and Lower Mississippi River Valley coming to Poverty Point (as exemplified in the artifacts present at the site [Gibson 2001, 2007; see also Pauketat and Sassaman 2020 for a review]), but also mound-building traditions seem to suggest some sort of social continuity between the Middle Archaic and Poverty Point; the historical knowledge of earthmoving is maintained over many generations and embedded in the landscape (see Sassaman 2005).

Today, it is generally accepted that Poverty Point was a multicultural space (see Kidder 2002; Kidder and Sassaman 2009; Sassaman 2005; Spivey et al. 2015), but previous theories focused on Poverty Point as a "closed society" and regional center (Gibson 2007), a place intermittently populated for trade (Jackson 1991), or as a mechanism for reducing population size – the focus on building (or producing) mounds diverted human energy away from repro-duction (Hamilton 1999). The latter idea has fallen out of favor. Yet none of these theories, according to Spivey et al. (2015), does justice to the dynamism that was Poverty Point. This place was unlike anything in the region. Poverty Point was important to the peoples who called it home but also to the broader historical context of the mound-building peoples of the Eastern Woodlands. For example, the earliest occupations of Poverty Point (c. 3600–3400 cal BP) were marked by inhabitants importing lithic materials, specifically Burlington chert, which is sourced from St. Louis, Missouri area, and a fan favorite of Mississippians who later built and populated Cahokia (Spivey et al. 2015). After this initial phase, the rings and mounds of Poverty Point were built as discussed earlier. But the novelty of cherts from faraway lands (in excess of 500 km) persisted into the later occupations and "can be measured in metric tons" (Gibson 2001; Spivey et al. 2015: 153).

This is a remarkable dedication to the obtainment of lithic materials from far-flung areas suggesting extensive utilization of trade networks and importation of goods. Exportation of Poverty Point goods is limited to the baked-clay objects referred to as Poverty Point Objects (some found as far-flung as north-western Florida [Hays et and Weinstein 2010]) and jasper owl beads (Spivey et al. 2015). The limited exportation of goods and intensive importation of lithics in addition to the variability in material culture present at Poverty Point suggests to Spivey et al. that Poverty Point was created through "an inwardly driven process, drawing people and raw materials to the site from across the

Southeast" Spivey et al. (2015: 154–155; but see also Sassaman 2005 for a similar idea). And furthermore, the "massive construction projects undertaken at Poverty Point after c. 3400 cal B.P. were about creating or re-creating a new, shared cosmology and cultural narrative" to unite persons with "varied geographic, ethnic, or social origins" (Spivey et al. 2015: 155). Poverty Point was a complex place populated by fisher-hunter-gatherers undergoing major social, political, and economic transformations leading to the development of "strong group identities" perhaps embodied in the construction of the mounds and ridges of Poverty Point (Spivey et al. 2015: 156; see also Anderson 2004; Anderson and Sassaman 2012; Sassaman 2010). Thus, Poverty Point was not just a place of trade and exchange, but rather a transformative event built upon the rich histories of mound building and earthmoving of the Eastern Woodlands and developed out of a shared sense of connection to place.

Middle Woodland c. 500 BCE– 400 CE

Following Poverty Point, some 1,000 years later, came the mound-building traditions of Adena and Hopewell – Adena being the earlier of the two (c. 500 BCE). Located in the Midwest, these two closely related traditions, for one, built mounds for mortuary purposes. Burying the dead in mounds was an elaborate process that involved the construction of a subterranean log-covered crypt that housed bodies and extravagant objects often from faraway places. Adena and Hopewell communities also built ritual buildings like charnel houses that protected the dead prior to burial mounds. They created elaborate mound enclosures marking complex astronomical alignments and built effigy mounds. These societies maintained their hunter-gatherer roots but began to rely on garden plots and early domesticated crops like *Chenopodium* (an oily, starchy seed like Quinoa), marsh elder, sunflower, and bottle gourd (see Fritz 2019). There is little convincing evidence that Middle Woodland groups ever fully embraced sedentism, yet the investment in mound building does emphasize a unique tie to landscape (Henry and Barrier 2016; but see Pacheco et al. 2020 for a different perspective). Perhaps participating in the building of these monumental earthworks was a way for Middle Woodland peoples to feel rooted in a place while maintaining a seminomadic lifestyle.

Many scholars (see Abrams and Freter 2005; Carr and Case 2005; Charles and Buikstra 2006; Clay 1998, 2014; Lynott 2015; Webb and Snow 1945) prefer to separate Adena (500 BCE– 250 CE) and Hopewell (200 BCE– 500 CE) into two distinct cultural groups based on geographic expansiveness. But, following Henry (2017: 190, 2018, 2020a,b), it is perhaps better suited to view these two groups as part of a broader regional history and one that emphasized the important processes of "memory as relational attachments" encompassing a diversity of people and places. The overlapping trajectories of these two complexes make it difficult to examine the two separately, as both communities shared "a coherent ideology—comprised primarily of animistic cosmological themes" and a penchant for mound building (Henry 2018; Henry and Barrier 2016; see also Beck and Brown 2012; Brown 1997, 2006; Carr and Case 2005; Case and Carr 2008). That said, the following summaries focus on aspects of each mound-building group as related to their locations in the Midwest and their social and cultural influence, of which the Hopewell seemingly surpassed that of Adena.

The Adena tradition is largely confined to the central Ohio Valley and parts of Indiana, Kentucky, West Virginia, and Pennsylvania and is best known for its very large conical earthen mortuary mounds, the largest of which is Grave Creek in West Virginia. Some 90 m in diameter and 21 m in height, this mound exemplifies the accretional technique of mound building used during this period; as persons continued to come back to these places, they added more earth. Large, circular post structures were located at the base of these mounds, built, used, and sometimes burned prior to the construction of the mound itself. Each successive mound surface was topped with a circular building, again burned or razed prior to the addition of more mound layers. In some cases, smaller mounds (like site 15Mm7 at the Wright Mounds) were potentially built in a single episode (Henry and Barrier 2016; see Webb 1940). In addition to the presence of conical mortuary mounds and circular post structures are raised circular earthen embankments. Their use, like the circular poststructures, is unknown, but some see these embankments as part of a broader ritual landscape (Clay 1998; Henry et al. 2020a). This landscape was created by the construction and association of conical mounds with circular embankments often situated *in between* different community settlements. The connections among kin-based coalitions are central to understanding the social relations born out of these landscapes (Henry and Barrier 2016). Mounds and embankments were, perhaps, not territorial markers but instead places marking corporate resources – whether those resources were ritual, social, or otherwise (Clay 1992; see also Henry and Barrier 2016; Pauketat and Sassaman 2020; Railey 1991). And furthermore, these places were tied to kin-based sodalities through the objects and materials that traveled along with the people themselves. Adena, much like Hopewell, trafficked in ritual objects.

The materiality of Adena was lavish and included carved stone tablets, groundstone celts and axes, hematite, and objects crafted from mica, as well as copper beads, bracelets, rings, and gorgets. Many of these objects were recovered from archaeological excavations of burials and exemplify zoomorphic motifs that continue into the Hopewell period (see Carr and Case 2005). Some of these motifs include birds, wolves, deer, and bears and occur as actual body parts present alongside their human counterparts in Adena burials. Perhaps most famous is the presence of modified wolf palates found with human remains in the Wright (the larger mound 15Mm6) and Ayers mounds; these palates featured intact incisors and canines cut to fit inside a human mouth (Webb and Baby 1957). The intimacy shared between human and animal was embodied by moments when a person (or persons) was perhaps engaged in a transformative process. Donning such a wolf palate likely created a new being, one with a new authority or power supernatural in nature (see Giles 2010; Wallis 2011). These relationships between the human and the other-than-human speak to the ways power was experienced in Adena communities. Heterarchical relationships valued persons within their "kin- ordered coalitions [and] permitted temporary opportunities for individuals to gain influence or to wield authority" emphasizing diversity of roles and social organization geared toward consensus building (Henry and Barrier 2016: 103).

Not dissimilar from the Adena, the Hopewell tradition (c. 200 BCE) is perhaps best understood as one of the most unique cultural groups in North America. Its religious traditions, earthworks, community settlements, and vast exchange networks created one of the most recognizable pre-European contact societies marked by what is generally understood as a shared and monolithic set of practices. Recent archaeological research has shown, however, that Hopewell should not be demarcated based on interregional connections among communities alone (à la Caldwell 1964), but instead on the local experiences of various communities (Carr 2005; Henry and Miller 2020; see also Byers and Wymer 2010; Carr and Case 2005; Charles and Buikstra 2006). To truly understand Hopewell, one must examine how local actors engage with (and perhaps transform) larger pan-regional themes (see Baires 2020; Henry and Miller 2020).

Like Adena, Hopewell culture emphasized the burial of the dead in earthen mounds, crypts, and charnel houses. They built mounds and were semisedentary. But what sets Hopewell apart is the construction of numerous geometric earthworks distributed over hundreds of square kilometers. These earthworks have been the focus of archaeological research since Squier and Davis (1848) first documented their breadth in shape, size, and orientation. Purposes of these enclosures are debated (see Bernardini 2004; Byers 2006), but it is generally accepted that they served as gathering places for perhaps thousands of people who likely did not live at these enclosures but resided in small villages away from the mounds (see Cowan 2006; Dancey and Pacheco 1997). Coming to these earthworks for, perhaps, "rituals of world renewal" emphasized these places as "instruments of social action whose engagement may have been routinized in ritual practice" embodied by the "material effects" that brought large numbers of people (Beck and Brown 2012; Giles 2010; Pauketat and Sassaman 2020: 326; see also Byers 1996). A sign of this "material effect" is the roads and pathways that connected some of these enclosures marking celestial alignments tied to the sun and/or the moon (Romain 2000; see also Hively and Horn 2013, 2019). The celestial alignments, as Romain (2015b) argues, of key earthen enclosures and the Great Hopewell Road are an earthly incarnation of the Path of Souls (represented by the Milky Way constellation [see Lankford 2007]), which guides the dead to their final resting place. This argument of celestial alignments as made material in the earthen landscape is compelling in that it accounts for a deep interconnection among Hopewell sites across vast distances citing the importance of movement through this landscape.

One other aspect worth mentioning here is the emphasis on movement not only of persons but also of things. Perhaps, Hopewell is most well-known for its extensive networks of trade and exchange dubbed the Hopewell-Interaction Sphere (Struever and Houart 1972; see Lepper 2006 for a summary). This network extends far beyond the central hub of Hopewell in Ohio to the Appalachia Mountains, Yellowstone, the Great Lakes, and the Gulf Coast. Objects made of mica, obsidian, copper, quartz crystal, pipestone, and other materials constitute the variety of things Hopewellian persons crafted and moved along community networks. Finished objects include (but this list is not exhaustive) copper jewelry, mica mirrors, copper cutouts shaped into geometric forms, human silhouettes, parts of animals, human figurines made from clay, platform pipes made from stone, and pottery vessels made in the likeness of zoomorphic figures; as William Dancey puts it, this list "includes everything in the natural world ... with an emphasis on things that glitter" (2005: 114). The purpose of these objects is often tied to a dynamic ritual practice among Hopewell peoples whose cosmology welcomed a Shamanistic tradition and rich mortuary culture (see Brown 2006; Carr and Case 2005).

Medieval Mississippian Communities c. 900–1500 CE

I admit I am skipping over the details of some 500 years of history to move us rapidly into the Medieval Mississippian period to examine Cahokia within the context of its contemporaries. To be clear, the previous 500 years are not devoid of mound-building histories and, in fact, carry some strikingly significant transformations to communities in the Midwest and Southeast. These include a reliance on corn brought up from the Southwest (Fritz 2019) leading to more sedentary village life, an emphasis on pottery as a marker of identity, as well as the introduction and adoption of the bow and arrow (Pauketat and Sassaman 2020: 377 for a summary). Not to mention the continuation of mound building at key sites like Troyville (in Louisiana), Toltec (in Arkansas), and Feltus (in Mississippi) along with the effigy mound-building cultures of the upper Midwest (see Kassabaum 2021; Nassaney 1994; Rees and Lee 2015; Steponaitis et al. 2015). These communities have real impacts on Mississippian cultural trajectories ushering in a transformative process based on ritual practice that involved mass human burials, the construction and use of new types of ritual architecture, massive post monuments, and the introduction of new types of personal adornment (particularly an emphasis on cloth production (see Alt 1999; see Pauketat and Sassaman 2020 for a review). This period was wedged between the socially transformative moments of the excess of the Middle Woodland and the beginnings of city life of the Mississippian whereby Late Woodland societies became "agents of change" moving the historical trajectories of Eastern Woodlands peoples toward new futures (Rees and Lee 2015: 195; see also Randall and Sassaman 2017).

This leads us to the Medieval Mississippian world (see Pauketat and Alt 2015) created (in part) by the Medieval Climatic Anomaly (c. 800–1300) that brought rain and warmth (raising temperatures by about 2°F) to the Midwest and Southeast (Benson et al. 2009; Pauketat 2020). The convergence of these moments led to the emergence of some of the largest Native North American communities north of Mexico prior to European colonization. Building on the rich histories and events of the previous years (from the Archaic all the way to the Late Woodland) Moundbuilders continued to modify the landscape in ways that foregrounded new ideas all while incorporating hints of traditions we should be familiar with by now. And particularly those that emphasize a deep tie to the land in ways that draw forth the elements (e.g., earth, water, and wood) needed and used in the construction of new urban-built environments. If Cahokia is conceived of as a "central place" or "place of origin" (following Baltus and Baires 2020), then we may look at its contemporaries as places that cite (either through material objects, building styles, pottery, and/or food grown and consumed) this city in and through the landscape. To exemplify this, I discuss the following sites: Trempealeau and Aztlan (in Wisconsin), Angel Mounds (in Indiana), Shiloh Mounds (in Tennessee), Moundville (in Alabama), and Etowah (in Georgia). While there are countless other Mississippian sites that can be considered contemporaneous and/or overlap with Cahokia, the aforementioned towns (none were ever as dramatic in size as Cahokia) capture the geographical expansiveness and cultural legacy of this particular period. My omission of other sites in no way downplays their importance to this moment in history, but rather speaks to the breadth and influence of Mississippian communities in the Eastern Woodlands.

Midwest: Trempealeau, Aztalan, and Angel

The Midwest, known for its vast farm fields, rich river valleys, and rolling topography is home to not only the city of Cahokia but also the important sites of Aztalan, Trempealeau, and Angel – all popping up around 1050–1100 CE. These three places provide a unique view into the ways the Cahokian "phenomenon" was experienced outside of the American Bottom and also shed light on how the message of this city traveled. Trempealeau, for example, is of particular interest. Located some 900 river km up the Mississippi River in Wisconsin, Trempealeau, dates to the very early days of Cahokia – 1050 CE. Described by Pauketat et al. (2015b) as a "shrine complex" and created by Cahokians, Trempealeau sat amid local Late Woodland Wisconsin communities. Access to this site from the American Bottom required an extensive and likely arduous trip *up* the Mississippi River. Boszhardt et al. argue that "the Cahokian migrants knew about their final destination before leaving, because so far no early Mississippian settlements are known to have existed between Cahokia and Wisconsin that might have served as way stations during the long trek north" (2015: 68). Cahokian travelers intended to arrive at the Trempealeau locale, and particularly the area that would become the mounded "shrine complex" of Little Bluff, right around 1050 CE. To set up this small community, Cahokians brought with them their own pottery, stone tools, and ways of doing things (see Boszhardt et al. 2015; Pauketat et al. 2015b). But why Trempealeau? Why travel by canoe up a dangerous river for hundreds of kilometers to a foreign place? Perhaps the draw of the Driftless Area (geomorphologically unique region of the Upper Midwest covered in rugged and forested landscapes with rock shelters and craggy springs [see Boszhardt 2003, 2004; Boszhardt et al. 2015; Emerson and Hughes 2000]) was enough? Or perhaps the knowledge of the effigy mound-building groups who created landscapes populated by animal and humanoid earthen mounds already identified this place as one entangled with "the spirits and elemental powers resident therein" (Pauketat et al. 2015b: 262). According to Pauketat et al. (2015b), the answer is yes to both abovementioned questions. Trempealeau served as a pivotal mission site, a place to share the Cahokian worldview with persons outside of the American Bottom by drawing on the "regions special properties or powers" (Pauketat et al. 2015b: 261; see also Alt and Pauketat 2015) experienced simultaneously in both the natural topography and the mounds visible in that northern landscape.

The sites of Little Bluff and the broader Trempealeau locale (Pauketat et al. 2017a) are uniquely situated atop the Trempealeau Bluffs – "a series of rugged loess-capped limestone and sandstone isolates in a broad floodplain adjacent to the modern-day Village of Trempealeau, Wisconsin" (Pauketat et al. 2015b: 262; see also Pauketat et al. 2017a). Due to its location in the floodplain, the bluffs appear to rise out of the Mississippi River some 30-m high surrounded, at its base, by "discontinuous occupation areas" (Pauketat et al. 2015b: 262) with evidence for red-slipped pottery (first identified by Squier 1905, 1917; see also Pauketat et al. 2015b) – a hallmark of Cahokian ceramic wares. These red-slipped wares were accompanied by other nonlocal items such as imported chert (raw material for making stone tools) and chunkey stones (stone discoidals used to play the game of Chunkey [see Zych 2015b]) along with wall-trench housing construction techniques unique to Cahokia (see Alt and Pauketat 2011). Furthermore, the Moundbuilders of Little Bluff followed mound construction practices utilized at Cahokia proper, which included "two distinct mounded areas dating to a span of mere decades, the largest and possibly earliest being a yellow-and-black layered bilaterally symmetrical mound-and-causeway monument topped by at least one shrine house with a yellow-and-black plastered hearth and floor" (Pauketat et al. 2015b: 283). In addition, two of the three mounds on Little Bluff are lunar aligned (Pauketat et al. 2017a: 192), something seen at Cahokia along with similar "shrine complexes" in the American Bottom (Alt 2013; Pauketat 2013a; see also Alt 2019).

It is clear from this archaeological evidence that in the early days of Cahokia's emergence, some of its citizens made their way up to this little spot on the Mississippi River to claim the powers of the landscape and to share their religious beliefs. This is embodied by the construction and use of a "shrine complex referencing the cosmos (specifically, the moon)," which includes the mounded landscape, and the intentional maintenance of Cahokia lifeways embodied in the use of Cahokian pots, cherts, and building techniques (Pauketat et al. 2015b: 284). Furthermore, there is no evidence of conflict between local peoples and this Cahokian entourage suggesting that Cahokians were welcomed upon arrival or at the very least tolerated by local Late Woodland communities (Boszhardt et al. 2015; Pauketat et al. 2015b). Trempealeau was essential to the founding of Cahokia. This place expanded the city's reach beyond the American Bottom drawing into the Cahokia realm all the powers the Driftless area had to offer, not to mention serving as a useful place to disseminate Cahokia's own religious message: one focused on the entanglement of human and other-than-human persons with the land and the cosmos (Pauketat et al. 2015b: 285).

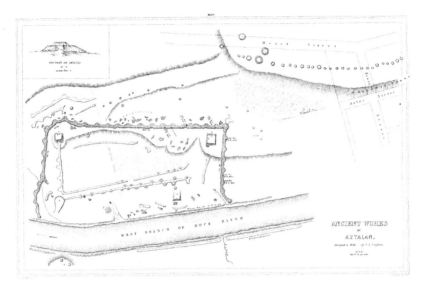

Figure 9 Aztalan, surveyed in 1850 by I. A. Lapham

Another important site in Wisconsin is Aztalan (c. 1100–1200 CE; a Late Woodland population was living in the area at 900 CE) located east of Madison on the west bank of the Crawfish River (Richards and Zych 2018; Figure 9). Nathaniel Hyer and Increase Lapham once thought this place was a "citadel" and the original home to the Aztec of Mexico. Today, Aztalan is recognized as a prominent Mississippian town built among Wisconsin's Late Woodland effigy mound culture. Archaeologists (see Baerreis 1958; Goldstein and Freeman 1997; Goldstein and Richards 1991; Richards 2007; Richards and Jeske 2002) determined that Aztalan was established by a group of Middle Mississippians from Cahokia (or possibly from the greater American Bottom region) who moved up to Wisconsin around the same time as Cahokian emissaries moved into Trempealeau coinciding with the Lohmann and Stirling phases of Cahokia's emergence. The rectilinear mound shapes, open plaza space, and bastioned palisade wall contrast quite distinctly with the "curvilinear shapes" of the local effigy mound groups highlighting Aztalan's difference and emphasizing the Mississippian influence in the region (Pauketat and Sassaman 2020: 389). Another point worth noting here is, like Trempealeau's Little Bluff, the builders of Aztalan took advantage of the natural topography to construct this town in a "shallow, bowl-like landform" where the mounds stand out against a backdrop of "rolling hills that grade into a glacial ridge" overlooking the palisaded town (Richards and Zych 2018: 236).

Like the goings-on at Trempealeau, the Mississippians who moved into this area near the Crawfish River also introduced Cahokian pottery styles and lithic artifacts alongside the unique architecture of Cahokia, which included wall-trench building methods, T-shaped structures, and earthen platform mound construction techniques (see Richards and Zych 2018 for a summary). Built on top of a Late Woodland village, Aztalan consists of three earthen platform mounds, one modified "gravel knoll" dubbed the "southeast mound" by Lynn Goldstein (2015), a central plaza area, and two palisade walls (likely built at different times) where the outer wall encircled an area of 9 ha (Zych 2015a; Richards and Zych 2018). The platform mounds seem to "occupy the four interior corners of a roughly rectangular space centered on an open plaza . . . [which suggest] Aztalan's site structure can be seen as reflective of the general Mississippian tendency toward quadripartition of space" representing the concept of the "four-cornered" world (Emerson 1997; Richards and Zych 2018: 238). This site orientation reflects the understanding that Cahokian-influenced landscapes exemplify politico-religious beliefs embodied in the construction and use of mound-and-plaza spaces (see Baires 2017a for review; Pauketat 2013a). As Zych (2015a: 55) states, the interactions between Middle Mississippians and local Late Woodland populations at Aztalan resulted in "discrete changes in the arrangement of the physical and social landscape" where Mississippian practices became directly incorporated into the preexisting center of a local Late Woodland village. This manifests in the literal construction of platform mounds and at the Northeast Mound that followed the decommissioning and relining (using yellow sand) of a large Late Woodland single-post structure – a practice common to the Cahokia area (Zych 2015a; see also Baltus and Baires 2012; Pauketat 2008). Additionally, a particularly unique piece of Aztalan's landscape is a series of ten conical mounds located about 170 m to the west of the northwest corner of the palisade, once part of a string of such mounds extending for about one-fourth of a mile (Richards and Zych 2018; see also Lapham 1850). Some of these mounds likely supported marker posts (hence them being dubbed "Marker Mounds") and at least one contained a burial of a female wrapped in shell beads, not unlike the famous "beaded blanket burial" of Cahokia's Mound 72 (Barret 1993; Richard and Zych 2018; see also Fowler et al. 1999).

Aztalan embodies the desire of Middle Mississippian peoples to explore and establish new communities and share new cultural beliefs and practices supported by the sustained mingling of Mississippians and local Late Woodland communities. Furthermore, the historical use of the Aztalan site area stretches back into the Archaic period (Richards 1992; Sampson 2008; see also Zych 2015a) indicating that as we have discussed for other regions, landscapes of human occupation *are citational* and powerful because of their long histories of use. For example, it is unclear if the string of conical mounds mentioned earlier were built by Late Woodland peoples or Middle Mississippians, but they likely connected the Aztalan inhabitants with a deeper understanding of the history of the landscape; as the mounds themselves were eventually adopted into the town plan of Aztalan, this history became part of a "new future" for the region, one steeped in Mississippian ways of being (see Randall and Sassaman 2017; Zych 2015a: 106). Similarly, the pottery of Aztalan indicates an exchange of ideas as evidenced by the incorporation of Cahokian-style ceramics (like Ramey), and the invention of hybrid styles utilizing Mississippian ceramic forms made from a local grit-tempered paste (Richards 1992; see also Richards and Zych 2018). Cahokian-style building methods and architectural styles are also seen at Aztalan, and furthermore, human bone chemistry evidence indicates a small number of sampled individuals were nonlocal, likely coming from the American Bottom or Illinois River Valley (Price et al. 2007).

Another Midwestern mound-town that features prominently in the "global" Mississippian world is Angel Mounds. Located along the banks of the Ohio River, east of modern-day Evansville, Indiana, the Angel Site consisted of eleven earthen mounds enclosed by multiple iterations of semicircular palisade walls along with a village component dubbed the "East Village" (Black 1967; see Watts Malouchos 2020a for a summary). Extensively excavated under the direction of Glenn A. Black in the 1930s until his unexpected death in 1964, Angel was cast as a Middle Mississippian Town dating from AD 1300 to AD 1600 (Black 1967: 549; see also Hilgeman 2000). With all the trappings of Mississippian cultural practice, Angel had platform mounds, wall-trench architecture, and artifact types and styles traceable to Cahokia (see Watts Malouchos 2020a for a review). However, Angel also exhibited its own unique histories beginning much earlier than AD 1300 and marked by the presence of Yankeetown (Late Woodland culture locale to the Angel region) ceramics at sites in Cahokia's Richland uplands, an extensive area in the uplands of Illinois, home to small farming villages of local and nonlocal peoples (see Alt 2002, 2006, 2019). The presence of Yankeetown peoples can also be traced to the sites of Cahokia, East St. Louis, and BBB Motor (a small ritual/religious site located on the northeastern boundary of Cahokia proper), indicating that those local to southwestern Indiana were likely part of the creation of this Native American city (Bareis and Porter 1984; Brennan 2016; Pauketat 2004; Watts Malouchos 2020b). The presence of Late Woodland Yankeetown peoples in the American Bottom region right at the emergence of Cahokia possibly contributes uniquely to the emergence of Angel. Perhaps "some of them, now newly Cahokianized, set up the new center of Angel" bringing back to Indiana Cahokian lifeways that

included methods of mound building and the knowledge of lunar alignments –
used both at Angel and at Cahokia to organize site layout (Pauketat and
Sassaman 2020: 402).

Recent archaeological work at Angel has extensively pushed back Black's
previous understanding of the occupational timeline of the site, aligning more
with theories presented by Alt (2002, 2006, 2012) and Pauketat and Sassaman
(2020) that potentially includes the involvement of "newly Cahokianized"
Yankeetown people in the process of building this town. Recent research
(Monaghan et al. 2013; Monaghan and Peebles 2010; Peterson 2010) provides
data in support of an Angel-founding event right around AD 1050 – the same
timeline we see for Trempealeau, Aztalan, and Cahokia itself. Yet, with Angel,
it is generally understood that only a small population inhabited the site or
possibly that it was not inhabited at all serving as a vacant ceremonial center
perhaps with just enough people to construct the two earthen platform mounds:
A and F (Monaghan and Peebles 2010; see also Hilgeman 2000; Peterson 2010;
see also Watts Malouchos 2020b). The construction of mounds A and F aligned
Angel to its cosmological axis tied to lunar alignments (Pauketat 2017; see
Romain 2014, 2019). Importantly, this orientation seems to follow "the foundational Cahokian cosmography, perhaps tapping into the more ancient Woodland
period cosmologies that associate the moon with fertility and female powers"
(Watts Malouchos 2020b: NP; see also Pauketat and Alt 2018). Pauketat (2017:
11) equates Angel with the "shrine complexes" of Trempealeau and Emerald
Mounds (located in the Richland uplands east of Cahokia) arguing that the
combination of the mound alignments with the later enclosure of the site in an
irregular semicircle palisade wall suggests that "the Angel site plan might even
be a monumental depiction of a half moon" (see also Romain 2015a).

While Pauketat (2017; see also Alt 2002, 2006, 2012; Watts Malouchos
2020b) suggests that Angel was a product of Cahokia, or at least minimally
influenced by it, we must also recognize Angel's uniqueness as evidenced by the
negative painted pottery present at the site. Negative painted pottery (NPP) "is
a rare prehistoric ceramic type that is decorated with a resist painting technique,
which creates a lighter- colored design outlined by a black pigment" (Baumann
et al. 2013: 221). NPP is found at archaeological sites throughout the Upper
South, with concentrations of it located in the Lower Ohio River Valley, the
Nashville Basin, and in the Bootheel of Missouri (see Hilgeman 2000; Morse
and Morse 1983; Phillips 1970). Pottery styles include plates, bowls, and bottles
with designs that include bounded triangular areas to nested diamonds and
chevrons (see Baumann et al. 2013). NPP is rare, and when it is found at
a site, it is almost always less than 1 percent of the total ceramic assemblage
(Hilgeman 2000). At Angel, NPP manifests in plate form with negative painting

designs (sun circle and cross in circle) present on plate rims (Hilgeman 1991, 2000; see also Baumann et al. 2013). Other forms of NPP at Angel follow the styles identified at Kincaid Mounds (Mississippian town in southern Illinois) and from the Nashville Basin (in Nashville Tennessee; Baumann et al. 2013). While originally thought to be a strictly ritual vessel type based on its paucity in domestic contexts, at Angel, NPP seems most heavily concentrated in the households and middens of the East Village (Baumann et al. 2013: 241). This is what makes the presence of NPP unique at Angel. Based on Hilgeman's (2000) research, Baumann et al. (2013) suggest that Angel's negative painted plates served two functions: public ceremonies and feasts, and private family rituals. The presence of NPP ceramics in the style of the Nashville Basin and Ohio River Valley indicates the possibility of peoples either migrating into Angel from those areas or the establishment of trade relationships (see Baumann et al. 2013; Hilgeman 2000). Either way, NPP made its way to Angel, and its uses were reimagined for a domestic context. By about AD 1200, anywhere between 200 and 3,000 people may have lived at Angel and the first outer palisade wall went up (Krus 2016; Peterson 2010; Watts Malouchos 2020b). Angel was abandoned by AD 1400, a theory supported by radiocarbon dating from two capping events on Mounds A and F (Monaghan and Peebles 2010: 950). Angel presents a unique case study for understanding the relationships Mississippian communities held with Cahokia. As Watts Malouchos puts it, "it was not the mere presence or ownership of Cahokian-made objects that perpetuated connections to Cahokia, rather it was the entangling of local communities (human and non-human constituents alike) with Cahokian cosmic powers" (2020b).

Southeast: Shiloh, Moundville, and Etowah

As you leave the Midwest, multiple prominent Middle Mississippian mound towns sit along the Tennessee and Cumberland Rivers. One of these Shiloh Mounds located on the Tennessee River in south-central Tennessee was a midsize fortified village occupied year-round. Early dates suggest occupation took place at the beginning of the Late Woodland period, with mound building occurring from AD 1100 to AD 1300 (Kidder and Sherwood 2017; see also Anderson et al. 2013; Welch 2006). Shiloh covered about 22 ha and was enclosed on the west side by a 900-m-long palisade wall; to the north and the south, the site was protected by steep-sided ravines (Welch 2006). The town itself consisted of 8 mounds and at least 100 houses all clustered around a central plaza. In addition, smaller farming hamlets were located outside the town walls in the surrounding river floodplain (Welch 2006). Perhaps the most impressive feature of this landscape was platform Mound A situated on a terrace edge 30 m above the Tennessee River. Mound A measured about 6.7 m high and 36.5 m in diameter (Kidder and Sherwood 2017). Today, the eastern margin of Mound A is eroding due to the "modern impoundment of the Tennessee River" undercutting the terrace edge (Kidder and Sherwood 2017: 12). This sparked a series of excavations that began in 1999 to salvage the eroding mound face and protect the remainder of the terrace edge (Anderson et al. 2013). Excavations revealed a highly complex mound construction history for Mound A that includes at least four stages of mound building along with 9 structures and relatively few artifacts (Anderson et al. 2013). Furthermore, Mound A includes layers of a unique and difficult-to-locate red-colored clayey sand (Kidder and Sherwood 2017: 15). One of the most impressive uses of this red clayey sand manifested as an extensive deposit some 20 cm thick. The sand was clean at the time of adding it to the mound and kept clean "suggesting this red surface signaled a specific function" (Kidder and Sherwood 2017: 16). It was on this red surface that the construction of the remainder of the mound continued. It is clear from the excavated profiles of Mound A that red clayey sands were intentionally chosen by the Shiloh Moundbuilders; the effort to obtain this pure red color would have been labor-intensive and important (see Kidder and Sherwood 2017; see also Pursell 2013). In fact, Corin Pursell (2013) suggests that projecting meaning through color was the point of Mound A. Using colored layers in mound construction would have been visible to Shiloh's inhabitants perhaps signaling certain "social conditions" as they changed over time (Pursell 2013: 84). While we cannot know for sure what those colors meant (but see Pursell 2013 for a hypothesis), what we do know is that it took substantial effort to construct these mounds with this color play in mind. From sourcing, the colored sediments to keeping them clean and pure indicate an intentionality associated with the processes of mound building. Much like we have seen with other societies from the Archaic to the Mississippian, mound building was never for function alone but entangled with expressive cultural knowledge emplaced upon the land.

Along the Black Warrior River in central Alabama sits the remains of one of the largest pre-Columbian settlements in the North American Southeast – Moundville (Figure 10). Beginning as a two-mound complex around AD 1120, Moundville grew to encompass some 325 acres with 29 earthen mounds and multiple households arranged around an open plaza for a population of about 1,000. This large mound-town was abutted by the Black Warrior River to the north and encircled by a 1 km long wooden palisade around the east, south, and west. Like Cahokia, Moundville was a "center-place" with a regional territory expanding into the heavily forested Gulf Coastal Plain. Farmers, like

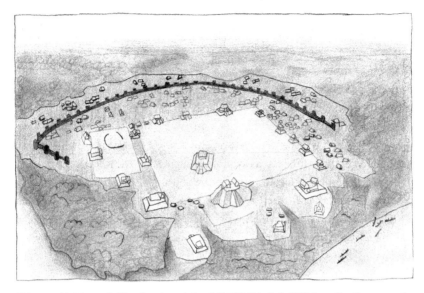

Figure 10 Moundville (by Aumich, CC BY-SA 3.0, Wikimedia Commons)

those at Cahokia, took advantage of the long summers and growing season to produce maize; hunters exploited natural resources like fish and turtles (see Blitz 2012 for a thorough review; see also Blitz 2008; Knight and Steponaitis 2006; Wilson 2008, 2010). Moundville enjoyed a long occupation (collapsing around AD 1600) that changed over time shifting from a fortified town to a ceremonial center. The town's early days, not unlike Cahokia's, were marked by a transition from the Terminal Late Woodland groups already living in the area to the Mississippian culture that eventually dominated the region. This is marked by the adoption of semisubterranean wall-trench houses, maize agriculture, and ceramic styles that utilize shell temper (se Blitz 2012; Jenkins 2003). However, Moundville peoples created a sort of "hybrid" community that retained "older indigenous Woodland traditions" while adopting "the new Mississippian practices, even among households at the same site" (Blitz 2012: 539).

After Moundville's initial founding moment, the community grew around AD 1200 to include multiple platform mounds, a central plaza, and a palisade wall. This expansion resulted in the complete razing of one of the first two mounds representing "an attempt by the emerging Moundville elite to selectively remove from the landscape any reminder of a particular political group's presence" (Wilson 2010: 8). Residential areas were created between the palisade and the plaza, and mounds were arranged from the largest (on the north end of the plaza) to the smallest (as you move out and around the plaza).

This indicates Moundville was a planned community – the builders had a design for their town, one focused on creating unique residential neighborhoods (see Knight and Steponaitis 2006; Peebles 1971, 1978). Between AD 1200 and AD 1300, ten distinct residential groups were spaced throughout the site "represented in the size and arrangement of paired earthen mounds around the central plaza" (Wilson 2010: 9). Each residential area was consciously maintained through the repeated rebuilding of structures to "delineate or inscribe a corporate kinship identity" (Wilson 2010: 9; see also Wilson 2008). As these residential groups increased in size, domestic space became more formally arranged to include the standardization of building practices creating workspaces, paths, and ritual areas (Wilson 2010: 10). After this 100-year period, Moundville transformed once again into a "necropolis" and vacant ceremonial center populated by a small number of elite and ritual specialists (Wilson 2010; see also Blitz 2012; Knight and Steponaitis 2006; Steponaitis 1998). This transition coincides with outmigration of Moundville people to the surrounding rural countryside that highlights a disjuncture with the previous ways of doing things. As Wilson (2010: 12) puts it, families no longer "raised buildings over the foundations of their parents and grandparents' homes" and instead Moundville became a place "steeped in mortuary ceremonialism." Marked by excess, this new mortuary ceremonialism included pottery bottles, ornaments of copper, shell, and stone "decorated with a new emphasis on representational art, such as bones, skulls, scalps, cross in circle, falcons, winged serpents and other symbols thought to represent concerns with ancestors, war, and death" (Blitz 2012: 542; see also Knight and Steponaitis 2006). After about AD 1400 burials declined along with the rich grave offerings of the previous years. Perhaps this indicated a loss of faith in an "old ideology," but once the burials ceased so too did the mound construction (Blitz 2012; Knight and Steponaitis 2006). As Moundville declined, six single-mound centers emerged nearby with new cemeteries and new, albeit smaller, communities. According to Blitz (2012: 542), "Moundville was no longer highly valued."

Located in what is now northern Georgia, the Mississippian mound-town of Etowah developed around AD 1100 (King 2003). Prior to Etowah's emergence, the areas of northern Georgia, southeastern Tennessee, and northeastern Alabama were "dominated by a series of social groups, each with a distinct material culture and history" (King 2012: 515; see also Cobb and King 2005; King 2003). Some of these groups relied on corn production and consisted of small, fortified community settlements. The location of these fortified communities in defensible areas suggests groups were familiar with conflict (King 2012). Etowah, according to King (2003, 2012), grew out of this unique social history drawing together new Mississippians to participate in earth renewal – a ceremony that brought people together in common purpose. King (2003, 2012: 516) cites the evidence of large feasting pits, quickly dug (likely for mound fill) and quickly filled (with food refuse) as indicative of large gatherings of people coming together to build Etowah's Mound A creating a space populated by diverse communities (documented by regional pottery styles) who, through participation in mound building, ensured continuance of their societies.

Sometime after AD 1250, Etowah was reimagined: mounds were enlarged, and Mound C was built. The residential area east of Mound A was leveled making space for a clay-lined plaza, and the entire site was fortified by a complex system of palisades, ditches, and borrow pits (Cobb and King 2005; King 2012). Burials became elaborate including fine objects of nonlocal origin and style including artwork symbolic of "mythical time" (Cobb and King 2005: 183). The reliance on the artwork, in a way, worked to create a new "ranked social order" based on a "system appealed to beliefs, imagery, and artwork that were foreign" to the region (Cobb and King 2005: 183). By about AD 1400, Etowah was abandoned, leaving smaller settlements in the valley and paving the way for a new political order, one witnessed by Hernando de Soto at the turn of the sixteenth century.

Historical Connections

Once Cahokia's population diminished transforming this once-great city into a vacant town c. AD 1350, the reverberations of this "collapse" could be felt throughout the Midwest and Southeast. Communities began engaging in warfare burning towns and targeting temples in the Mississippi Valley. Evidence from cemeteries in the Illinois River Valley indicates 40 percent of the women and men buried suffered violent deaths (Milner et al. 2013). As a result, people began to flee transforming this once rich landscape into a "Vacant Quarter" phasing out the Mississippian civilization in the American Bottom region (Cobb and Butler 2002; see also Buchanan 2015). Combined with the deterioration of the Mississippian stronghold on the area was the return of a new climactic anomaly that perhaps stressed these communities even more – the Little Ice Age. This brought about droughts and cold weather creating a less-than-ideal situation for growing corn (Peregrine 2020; see also Benson et al. 2009; Pauketat 2020b). People began moving into the Plains and the Deep South, some who would eventually meet Hernando de Soto as the Coosa Nation (see Blanton 2020; Hudson et al. 1985; Regnier 2014). The effect of the depopulation of Cahokia – the regions' once-grand melting pot of people, ideas, and practices – could be felt in the stressed "social fabric of the lower Mississippi Valley," which was likely exacerbated by the convergence of immigrants moving into newly established small towns (Pauketat and Sassaman 2020: 413). When European colonists arrived in the south in the sixteenth century, they were met by communities of people who transformed and adapted their Mississippian lifeways to create new nations or confederacies ruled, as we know from de Soto's accounts, by hereditary leaders (Hudson et al. 1985; see also Knight 2009; Wesson and Rees 2002). This new world order is perhaps most well known as the Coosa chiefdom, a highly complex society with a centralized leadership governing a series of smaller towns from northeastern Tennessee south to northern Georgia and into central Alabama (Hudson 1998; Hudson et al. 1985). While the Mississippian cultural zenith as tied to Cahokia was long gone, the historical connections to this place continued through legacies of land and tradition.

The review in this section serves two purposes: (1) to articulate the importance of mound building to the peoples of the Eastern Woodlands and (2) to contextualize the city of Cahokia within a broad historical trajectory. The Mississippian world of the Eastern Woodlands was entangled in a complex network of social histories that emphasized "glocal" (to borrow from Alice Wright 2020) connections in the creation of these new societies. The reverberations of this history embodied by Archaic and Woodland communities and the subsequent Mississippian city and towns can be felt beyond the colonial period. Their legacies remain in the landscapes modified to reflect their beliefs and politics and in the cultural traditions that laid the foundations for some of the historically known nations like the Choctaw, Muskogee, Chickasaw, and Osage (see Pauketat and Sassaman 2020). From here, we return to the idea of how these Mississippian communities become historicized recognizing that archaeological sites sit within an imaginary of the unique American cultural and historical narrative.

4 Historicizing the Cahokian World

Archaeological worlds in the Americas, as discussed at the outset of this Element, are often divided into two categories: prehistory and history. This division, critiqued by many (see Sassaman 2010 for review) stems from the colonial origins of the discipline where one of the featured goals of archaeology was to collect cultural resources of the "other" and bring them back for display in both private and public collections (see Gosden 1999). These collections often sought to compare "prehistoric" cultures at a global scale creating data sets that spoke to macroscale slow, evolutionary-cultural change. This is based on the idea that "Natives" were timeless and static – ultimately "without a history" (see Krupat 1995 for discussion). This process of collecting was an attempt at understanding and controlling the "other" in a time when Europeans focused on expanding empires that led to sometimes contentious encounters with drastically different groups of people. The collecting of materials, ideas, and persons, from these colonial encounters resulted in the hierarchical organization of human beings in comparison to their European colonizers. Thus, models of cultural evolution based on mass observations of the material world drove the origins of the discipline creating a framework striving to quantify human difference to make sense of the past and the present (see Gosden 1999: 30–32). American anthropological archaeology developed out of this drive for cross-cultural comparison, whereby "anthropology is fundamentally a generalizing and comparative discipline" with the goal of examining the processes of culture change (Willey and Sabloff 1980: 1; see also Gosden 1999: 4).

In the context of Native North American archaeology, these ideals fueled the Moundbuilder Myth, wherein early archaeologists examined the archaeological record for evidence of possible ancestral European origins for some of the earliest Native American sites (see Section 1; see also Trigger 1980). This Moundbuilder Myth led to early American governmental policies like the expansionist practices of the nineteenth century and the forced removal of Native Americans from their ancestral lands that followed. Emerging out of this moment, the evolutionary theory took hold of archaeological research creating a scholarly landscape that sought to highlight Native American cultures as quintessential examples of "Stone Age" culture. With this as its history, American archaeology developed into a discipline focused on studying the evolution of human culture to institutionalize broad generalizations about human behavior as it changed over time (Binford 1967). However, this left the "tricky question of the relationship between past and present forms of life" or rather how one can come to understand past human experience through an analysis of human variability in the present (Gosden 1999: 5). This issue brought about the use of analogy in archaeology (see Binford 1967, 1972) where examples from the present could be used as hypotheses to test past human behavior allowing archaeologists to create analyses that relied upon generalizations of human cultural practice. Ultimately, this research focused on notions of evolutionary change with a functionalist bent leaving much to be desired in terms of understanding the social experiences of past peoples.

I bring all this up as a backdrop to understanding how Native American cultures, experiences, and histories fit into the broader context of the history of the United States and more broadly into the divide between prehistory and history. This division stems from the development of the United States as a product of colonialism and the desire by early Euro-American archaeologists to discover some semblance of history they could latch on to in support of their continued domination of the Americas (see Wolfe 2006; see also Arjona 2015). But, ultimately this divide between prehistoric and historic articulates the idea that the "subjects of prehistory are the subjects of primitiveness" ultimately serving as a "benchmark against which human progress is measured" (Sassaman 2010: 22). If we were to accept the notion that Native American societies fall within this predetermined category of "primitiveness," then what to make of the thousands of years of archaeological data that speak to the highly complex social, political, and economic relationships identifiable through the material record (see Section 3)? Such categorizations are limiting to say the least and ultimately strip communities of their valuable histories – a political act (à la Robb and Pauketat 2013: 28; see also Povinelli 2016). As such, it is better suited to emphasize the very real importance of seeing Native American societies as embedded within a historical framework and one that views histories as "the ongoing process of making culture through social interactions" (Sassaman 2010: 26; see also Ethridge and Bowne 2020). This idea of history as "making culture" is closely tied to an understanding of the multiscalar processes of social change that emphasize "history as multiple genealogies of practices" (see Robb and Pauketat 2013: 26). These "genealogies of practice," then, are built by the intimate connections among place, person, and action that ultimately shape experiences and define histories. For example, if we think back to the Native American landscapes of the Eastern Woodlands as they were populated by diverse persons and experiences, practices of terraforming (e.g., making the natural landscape habitable for humans), mound building, mortuaries, and farming manifest as tangible historical moments that then become gathered and emplaced in landscapes of experience.

Ultimately, the past is populated by human (and other-than-human) experience that eschews arbitrary temporal boundaries and Western-derived categories of relatedness (see TallBear and Willey 2019b). This is something that Elizabeth Povinelli (2016: 27) deftly examines when she considers the ways Indigenous worldviews have been co-opted by postcolonial narratives that frame such beliefs and ways of life within the context of totemism. To move beyond these problematic categorizations is a difficult task, but one that requires a focus on the "analytics" of being, or rather the ways humans and other-than-humans "exist through an effort of mutual attention" (Povinelli 2016: 28). Archaeology of the Eastern Woodlands is much better suited to examining Native American histories as acts of bundling or "mutual attention" (Povinelli 2016) whereby "nodes in networks of meaning form the fabric of history" (Robb and Pauketat 2013: 28). This is a relational approach and one that sees actors as entangled in complex networks. These complex networks blur the boundaries of time and place, experience, and ontology.

Engaging with Native American pasts requires a reconceptualization of the processes of being as well as the experiences of time where each moment can be viewed as part of entwined genealogies of practices (Ingold 2007; see also Robb and Pauketat 2013). The settler-colonial history of what-is-now the United States does not readily recognize this kind of ontological understanding whereby concepts of relatedness reflect the dynamic nature of connections among the material, immaterial, human, and other-than-human actors in indigenous social worlds (see Shorter 2016; see also Povinelli 2016). Such an ontological perspective calls for "ontological attention to indigenous intersubjectivity" focused on the dynamic ways Indigenous people create and maintain diverse relations among persons (Shorter 2016). This requires an eschewing of a binary approach to the past that readily recognizes a division between "subject" or "object," "human" or "not human," "life" or "non-life"; instead (and following Indigenous scholars [see TallBear and Willey 2019b for a brief review; Povinelli 2016; Shorter 2016; Todd 2016]) archaeological investigations of the past must engage with social relations and occurrences as part of a "meshwork" (Ingold 2007) of experiences. These experiences have a material component that lives in the landscape, buildings, objects, bodies, and places that constitute the archaeological record. Finally, when Native American pasts are recognized *as history* this too is a political act, that one that re-centers the idea of what it means to be an "American" to include the thousands of years prior to the settler invasion of the North American continent.

A Cahokian History

Cahokia was a vibrant place situated in a crook of the Mississippi River, where fertile soils supported the growth of corn, sunflower, and chenopod (among other crops) and where those same soils supported the construction of some of the largest earthen mounds in North America. The bluff edges to the east led to the Richland uplands where migrants and locals forged new communities of farmers and craft workers connected to the heart of Downtown Cahokia through trade and tribute, politics, and belief. City dwellers built their wall-trench semisubterranean houses in alignment to Cahokia's five-degree offset organizational grid that provided order to not only the realm of daily living but also served as a connection to the cosmos, which featured prominently in the built landscape. Woodhenge marked the solstitial movements while the Rattlesnake Causeway and the alignments it afforded between Monks Mound and Rattlesnake Mound cited the moon and its subtle movements through the night sky (see Baires 2017a; see also Pauketat et al. 2015b; Romain 2015a). Meanwhile, the boroughs of St. Louis and East St. Louis followed their own strict organizational grids with buildings and mounds aligned to create the same affective qualities of Downtown Cahokia. These landscapes united the people of Cahokia through the dynamics of the built world where mounds, households, public buildings, and spaces all worked together in curating a unique urban experience. This rich landscape also included the powerful pairing of mounds with pools of water that perhaps in their juxtaposition embodied the myths of world creation and renewal while emphasizing the importance of water to the overall design of the city landscape (Baires 2015, 2017; see Pauketat 2020a). And while water is central to life because it is "life-giving," it is also a potent, fluid being with its own autonomy and agency. Water, in its multiple forms (creeks, ponds, lakes, the Mississippi River, rain, fog, and mist), was imperative to Cahokia's emergence both in its connections to stories of world creation (see Baires 2017a for a summary) and in its ability to sustain life through the growing of crops in surplus. Simultaneously, water distinguished the built landscape of this early city connecting things like the warm, moist weather to the needs of growing corn, as well as the ontological experience of watery places on the landscape as they organized the layout of this city (see Pauketat 2020a). Borrow pits, or places used to dig out the soils needed to build the mounds, were oftentimes intentionally left open (see Baires et al. 2017) to fill in with water, creating pools teeming with water lilies, waterfowl, fish, and amphibians. These watery places were part of steam-bath ceremonialism, which marked a quintessential practice of early Cahokia (Pauketat 2020a; see also Pauketat et al. 2017a). Water also appeared in more subtle forms in the use of freshwater shells as temper in pots (Pauketat et al. 2017a) and in the inclusion of marine shells with burials in ridgetop mounds (see Baires 2017a). Earthen causeways provided raised walkways through marshy landscapes connecting mounds, neighborhoods, and plazas (Baires 2017a; see also Pauketat 2020a). The Cahokian world was one steeped in water in all its forms; a centrally important element that permeated daily living through the iconography on pots, shell pottery tempers, shell cups and spoons, and shell gorgets and beads, landscape features, and weather patterns that brought the rains, thunderstorms, and potential for tornadoes the Midwest still experiences today.

This Native American city, in all its dynamism, is a place with a rich history embedded in a deep connection to place and tradition. As discussed in Section 3, such tradition goes back thousands of years to the Archaic period peoples who first began manipulating the soils and shells around them to create some of the earliest earthen mounds and shell rings. These edifices became markers of villages – perhaps some of the first on the North American continent (see

Thompson 2018). This historical moment led to Poverty Point, home to a complex arrangement of mounds in the shape of birds in flight, concentric rings, domes, and platforms all aligned along the edge of the Bayou Macon. This place has perhaps some of the earliest evidence demonstrating a multicultural community gathered to participate in the events of mound and community building, trade, and the exchange of ideas (see Sassaman 2005 for a review). Bringing us into the Middle Woodland, we see an explosion of mound building across the landscape of what is now Illinois, Ohio, and Kentucky (as well as some other more far-flung places like Arkansas and West Virginia) highlighting a culture of practice that involved an intimate knowledge of the earthly and celestial realms (see Carr and Case 2005). In addition, the Middle Woodland saw a boom of expansive trade networks with goods moving from the Great Lakes to the Rocky Mountains to the coastal south (see Struever and Houart 1972). The following Late Woodland period saw the traditions of effigy mound-building peoples in the Wisconsin driftless area (see Theler and Boszhardt 2000) as well as mound building at sites like Troyville in Louisiana, among others (see Kassabaum 2021; Nassaney 1994; Rees and Lee 2015; Steponaitis et al. 2015). These historical moments bring us into the Mississippian period marked by the emergence of the largest city north of Mexico – Cahokia. This cultural event did not happen in a historical vacuum, nor did it disappear when the Cahokia population dwindled in the late fourteenth century. We see perseverance of mound and community building well into the fifteenth century and at contact recognition of these mounded landscapes as centrally important to the historical happenings of the Eastern Woodlands.

Cahokia looms large over the Eastern Woodlands; it was the biggest place of its kind in both population and land coverage. However, Cahokia was no more or less important than the other cultural moments discussed earlier in the text. When we reflect upon history in the pre-Columbian Native American world, we must focus on "their distinctive relational fields ... in order to build better histories of the past" (Pauketat 2013b: 55). This means moments of continuity and change are part of the same social phenomenon recognizing that temporalities are layered and intertwined rather than linear. Additionally, these temporalities and histories are populated by agentic beings (not all of whom are human) that contribute to the shaping and mediating of those histories (see Pauketat 2013b; Povinelli 2016). These beings cross between archaeological time periods. Yes, the Archaic period is characterized by its own "set" of practices and events but these practices and events have far-reaching impacts that flow through the short-term to impact long-term processes of culture change. This is how Cahokia was created, through the nested and entangled strings of relationships that course through the landscape of the Eastern

Woodlands. What is perhaps particularly important in this conceptualization is that these tendrils of practice grow up through the soil like the first stalks of corn ushering in the diversity of these places while simultaneously tying them together through thousands of years of shared histories. Cahokia, and all the mounds, persons, and relationships that came before and after it, was (is) a pivotal part of the experiences of the North American continent and more specifically that of the Eastern Woodlands world. Visiting these mounded landscapes outside of settler notions of history and time require an active consideration of the relationships that built these places whereby the rules of cultural evolution do not and need not apply.

References

Abrams, E. M. and Freter, A. C. (eds.) (2005) *The Emergence of the Moundbuilders: The Archaeology of Tribal Societies in Southeastern Ohio*. Athens: Ohio University Press.

Alberti, B. (2016) "Archaeologies of Ontology," *Annual Review of Anthropology*, 45(1), pp. 163–179.

Alberti, B. *et al.* (2011) "'Worlds Otherwise': Archaeology, Anthropology, and Ontological Difference," *Current Anthropology*, 52(6), pp. 896–912. http://doi.org/10.1086/662027.

Alberti, B. and Marshall, Y. (2009) "Animating Archaeology: Local Theories and Conceptually Open-ended Methodologies," *Cambridge Archaeological Journal*, 19(3), pp. 344–356.

Alt, S. M. (1999) "Spindle Whorls and Fiber Production at Early Cahokian Settlements," *Southeastern Archaeology*, 18, pp. 124–133.

Alt, S. M. (2002) "Identities, Traditions, and Diversity in Cahokia's Uplands," *Midcontinental Journal of Archaeology*, 27(2), pp. 217–235.

Alt, S. M. (2006) "The Power of Diversity: The Roles of Migration and Hybridity in Culture Change," in Butler, B. M. and Welch, P. D. (eds.), *Leadership and Polity in Mississippian Society*. Carbondale: Southern Illinois University (Center for Archaeological Investigations, 33), pp. 289–308.

Alt, S. M. (ed.) (2010) *Ancient Complexities: New Perspectives in Precolumbian North America*. Salt Lake City: University of Utah Press (Foundations of Archaeological Inquiry).

Alt, S. M. (2012) "Making Mississippian at Cahokia," in Pauketat, T. R. (ed.), *The Oxford Handbook of North American Archaeology*. Oxford: Oxford University Press, pp. 497–508.

Alt, S. M. (2013) "A Tale of Two Temples," paper presented at the *57th Annual Meeting. Midwestern Archaeological Conference*, Columbus, Missouri.

Alt, S.M. (2018) Putting Religion ahead of Politics: Cahokian Origins as Viewed through Emerald's Shrines. In *Archaeology and Ancient Religion in the American Midcontinent*, edited by B.H. Koldehoff and T.R. Pauketat, pp. 208-233. University of Alabama Press: Tuscaloosa.

Alt, S. M. (2019) *Cahokia's Complexities: Ceremonies and Politics of the First Mississippian Farmers*. Tuscaloosa: University of Alabama Press.

Alt, S. M. and Pauketat, T. R. (2011) "Why Wall Trenches?," *Southeastern Archaeology*, 30(1), pp. 108–122.

Alt, S. M. and Pauketat, T. R. (2015) "The Elements of Cahokian Shrine Complexes and the Basis of Mississippian Religion," in Barber, S. and Joyce, A. (eds.), *Religion and Politics in the Ancient Americas*, pp 51–74. Boulder: University of Colorado Press.

Anderson, D. G. (2004) "Archaic Mounds and the Archaeology of Southeastern Tribal Societies," in Gibson, J. L. and Carr, P. J. (eds.), *Signs of Power: The Rise of Cultural Complexity in the Southeast*, pp. 270–299. Tuscaloosa: University of Alabama Press.

Anderson, D. G., Cornelison, J. E. Jr., and Sherwood, S. C. (eds.) (2013) *Archaeological Investigations at Shiloh Indian Mounds National Historic Landmark (40HR7) 1999–2004 Shiloh National Military Park Hardin County, Tennessee.* Tallahassee, FL: National Park Service Southeast Archaeological Center.

Anderson, D. G. and Sassaman, K. E. (2012) *Recent Developments in Southeastern Archaeology: From Colonization to Complexity.* Washington, DC: Society for American Archaeology.

Arjona, J. (2015) "Sublime Perversions: Capturing the Uncanny Affects of Queer Temporalities in Mississippian Ruins," *Journal of Social Archaeology*, 16(2), pp. 189–215.

Baerreis, D. A. (1958) "Aztalan Revisited: An Introduction," *The Wisconsin Archaeologist*, 2(4), pp. 5–20.

Atalay, Sonya (2016). "Engaging Archaeology: Positivism, Objectivity, and Rigor in Activits Archaeology" in *Transformiong Archaeology: Activist Practices and Prospects* edited by, Sonya Atalay, Lee Rains Clauss, Randall H McGuire, and John R. Welch. Routledge: New York, pp. 1–22.

Baires, S. E. (2015) "The Role of Water in the Emergence of the Pre-Columbian Native American City Cahokia" *Wiley Interdisciplinary Reviews: Water*, 2 (5), pp. 489–503.

Baires, S. E. (2017a) "A Microhistory of Human and Gastropod Bodies and Souls during Cahokia's Emergence," *Cambridge Archaeological Journal*, 27 (2), pp. 245–260.

Baires, S. E. (2017b) *Land of Water, City of the Dead Religion and Cahokia's Emergence.* Tuscaloosa: University of Alabama Press.

Baires, S. E. (2020) "Some Comments on Situations in the Midcontinental Middle Woodland," *Midcontinental Journal of Archaeology*, 45(3):1–16.

Baires, S. E. and Baltus, M. R. (2019) "Religious Partners: Material and Human Actors in the Creation of Early Cahokia," in Barrier, C. and Carmondy, S. B. (eds.), *Shamans, Priests, Practice, Belief: Archaeological Examinations of Ritual and Religion in the Eastern Woodlands*, pp., 166–167. Tuscaloosa: University of Alabama Press.

Baires, S. E., Baltus, M. R., and Malouchos, E. W. (2017) "Exploring New Cahokian Neighborhoods: Structure Density Estimates from the Spring Lake Tract, Cahokia," *American Antiquity*, 82(4), pp. 742–760.

Baltus, M. R. (2014) Transforming Material Relationships: 13th Century Revitalization of Cahokia Religious-Politics. PhD Dissertation, University of Illinois, Urbana-Champaign.

Baltus, M. R. and Baires, S. E. (2012) "Elements of Ancient Power in the Cahokian World," *Journal of Social Archaeology*, 12(2), pp. 167–192.

Baltus, M. R. and Baires, S. E. (2020) "Creating and Abandoning 'Homeland': Cahokia as Place of Origin," *Journal of Archaeological Method and Theory*, 27(1), pp. 111–127.

Barad, K. (2003) "Posthumanist Performativity: Toward an Understanding of How Matter Comes to Matter," *Signs: Journal of Women in Culture and Society*, 28(3), pp. 801–831.

Bareis, C. J. and Porter, J. W. (eds.) (1984) *American Bottom Archaeology: A Summary of the FAI-270 Project Contribution to the Culture History of the Mississippi River Valley*. Urbana: University of Illinois Press.

Barret, S. A. (1993) *Ancient Aztalan* Bulletin 12, Public Museum of the City of Milwaukee.

Baumann, T. E., Gerke, T. L., and Reber, E. A. (2013) "Sun Circles and Science: Negative Painted Pottery from Angel Mounds (12Vg1)," *Midcontinental Journal of Archaeology*, 38(2), pp. 219–244.

Beck, R. A. and Brown, J. A. (2012) "Political Economy and the Routinization of Religious Movements: A View from the Eastern Woodlands," *Archaeological Papers of the American Anthropological Association* (Beyond Belief: The Archaeology of Religion and Ritual, 1), 21(1)72–88.

Benchley, E. D. (2003) "Mississippian Alkali Processing of Corn," *Wisconsin Archaeologist*, 84, pp. 127–137.

Benson, L. V., Pauketat, T. R., and Cook, E. R. (2009) "Cahokia's Boom and Bust in the Context of Climate Change," *American Antiquity*, 74(3), pp. 467–483.

Bernardini, W. (2004) "Hopewell geometric earthworks: a case study in the referential and experiential meaning of monuments." *Journal of Anthropological Archaeology* 23(3): 331-356.

Betzenhauser, A. (2011) *Creating the Cahokian Community: The Power of Place in Early Mississippian Sociopolitical Dynamics*. Published PhD Dissertation. University of Illinois.

Betzenhauser, A. and Pauketat, T. R. (2019) "9 Elements of Cahokian Neighborhoods," *Archeological Papers of the American Anthropological Association*, 30(1), pp. 133–147.

Binford, L. R. (1967) "Smudge Pits and Hide Smoking: The Use of Analogy in Archaeological Reasoning," *American Antiquity*, 32, pp. 1–12.

Binford, L. R. (1968) "Some Comments on Historical versus Processual Archaeology," *Southwestern Journal of Anthropology*, 24(3), pp. 267–275.

Binford, L. R. (1972) *An Archaeological Perspective*. New York: Seminar Press.

Black, G. A. (1967) *The Angel Site: An Archaeological, Historical, and Ethnological Study*. Indianapolis: Indiana Historical Society.

Blanton, D. B. (2020) *Conquistador's Wake: Tracking the Legacy of Hernando de Soto in the Indigenous Southeast*. Athens: University of Georgia Press.

Blitz, J. H. (2008) *Moundville*. Tuscaloosa: University of Alabama Press.

Blitz, J. H. (2012) "Moundville and the Mississippian World," in Pauketat, T. R. (ed.), *The Oxford Handbook of North American Archaeology*. Oxford: Oxford University Press, pp. 534–546.

Boszhardt, R. F. (2003) *Deep Cave Rock Art in the Upper Mississippi Valley*. St. Paul, MN: Prairie Smoke Press.

Boszhardt, R. F. (2004) "The Late Woodland and Middle Mississippian Component at the Iva Site, La Crosse County, Wisconsin in the Driftless Area of the Upper Mississippi River Valley," *The Minnesota Archaeologist*, 63, pp. 60–85.

Boszhardt, R. F., Benden, D. M., and Pauketat, T. R. (2015) "Early Mississippian Outposts in the North," in Pauketat, T. R. and Alt, S. M. (eds.), *Medieval Mississippians: The Cahokian World*. Santa Fe, NM: School for Advanced Research Press, pp. 63–70.

Brecher, K. and Haag, W. G. (1983) "Astronomical Alignments at Poverty Point," *American Antiquity*, 48(1), pp. 161–163.

Brennan, T. K. (ed.) (2016) *Main Street Mound: A Ridgetop Monument at the Easter St. Louis Mound Complex*. Urbana-Champaign: Prairie Research Institute, University of Illinois (Illinois State Archaeological Survey Research Report, 36).

Brennan, T. K. *et al.* (2018) "Community Organization of the East St. Louis Precinct," in Emerson, T. E., Koldehoff, B. H., and Brennan, T. (eds.), *Revealing Greater Cahokia, North America's First Native City: Rediscovery and Large-Scale Excavations of the East St. Louis Precinct*, pp. 147–199. Champaign: University of Illinois Press (Illinois State Archaeological Survey Series, 12).

Brennan, T. K. (2021) "Making Mounds, Making Mississippian Communities in Southern Illinois," in Watts Malouchos, E. and Betzenhauser, A. (eds.), *Reconsidering Mississippian Communities and Households*, pp. 32–49. Tuscaloosa: University of Alabama Press.

Brown, J. A. (1997) "The Archaeology of Ancient American Religion in the Eastern Woodlands," *Annual Review of Anthropology*, 26, pp. 465–485.

Brown, J. A. (2006) "The Shamanic Element in Hopewell Period Ritual," in Charles, D. and Buikstra, J. (eds.), *Recreating Hopewell*. Gainesville: University Press of Florida, pp. 475–488.

Buchanan, M. E. (2015) "War-scapes, Lingering Spirits, and the Mississippian Vacant Quarter," in Buchanan, M. E. and Skousen, B. J. (eds.), *Tracing the Relational: The Archaeology of Worlds, Spirits, and Temporalities*. Salt Lake City: University of Utah Press, pp. 85–99.

Byers, A. M. (1996) *Cahokia: A World Renewal Cult Heterarchy*. Gainesville: University Press of Florida.

Byers, A. M. (1996) "Social Structure and the Pragmatic Meaning of Material Culture: Ohio Hopewell as Ecclesiastic-Communal Cult," in Pacheco, P. J. (ed.), *A View from the Core: A Synthesis of Ohio Hopewell Archaeology*. Columbus: Ohio Archaeological Council, pp. 174–192.

Byers, A. M. (2006) "Enclosures and Communities in Ohio Hopewell: An Essay," in Charles, D. and Buikstra, J. (eds.), *Recreating Hopewell*. Gainesville: University Press of Florida, pp. 74–105.

Byers, A. M. and Wymer, D. A. (eds.) (2010) *Hopewell Settlement Patterns, Subsistence, and Symbolic Landscapes*. Gainesville: University Press of Florida.

Caldwell, J. R. (1964) "Interaction Spheres in Prehistory," in Caldwell, J. R. and Hall, R. L. (eds.), *Hopewellian Studies*. Springfield: Illinois State Museum, pp. 133–143.

Carr, C. (2005) "Historical Insights into the Direction and Limitations of Recent Research on Hopewell," in Carr, C. and Case, T. (eds.), *Gathering Hopewell: Society, Ritual, and Ritual Interaction*. New York: Kluwer/ Plenum, pp. 51–70.

Carr, C. and Case, T. (2005) *Gathering Hopewell: Society, Ritual, and Interaction*. New York: Plenum.

Case, T. and Carr, C. (2008) *The Scioto Hopewell and Their Neighbors: Bioarchaeological Documentation and Cultural Understanding*. Berlin: Springer.

Chapman, Robert (2003) *Archaeologies of Complexity*. Routledge: London.

Charles, D. and Buikstra, J. (2006) *Recreating Hopewell*. Gainesville: University Press of Florida.

Claassen, C. (2010) *Feasting with Shellfish in the Southern Ohio Valley: Archaic Sacred Sites and Rituals*. Knoxville: University of Tennessee Press.

Claassen, C. (2011) "Shell Symbolism in Pre-Columbian North America," in Cakirlar, C. (ed.), *Archaeomalacology Revisited: Non-dietary Use of Molluscs in Archaeological Settings*. Oxford: Oxbow Books, pp. 230–236.

Clark, J. E. (2004) "Surrounding the Sacred: Geometry and Design of Early Mound Groups as Meaning and Function," in Carr, P. J. and Gibson, J. L. (eds.), *Signs of Power: The Rise of Cultural Complexity in the Southeast.* Tuscaloosa: University of Alabama Press, pp. 162–213.

Clark, P. (ed.) (2013) *The Oxford Handbook of Cities in World Archaeology.* Oxford: Oxford University Press.

Clay, R. B. (1992) "Chiefdoms, Big Men, or What? Economy, Settlement Patterns, and Their Bearing on Adena Political Models," in Seeman, M. F. (ed.), *Cultural Variability in Context: Woodland Settlements of the Ohio Valley.* Kent, OH: Kent State University Press, pp. 77–80.

Clay, R. B. (1998) "The Essential Features of Adena Ritual and Their Implications," *Southeastern Archaeology,* 17(1), pp. 1–21.

Clay, R. B. (2014) "What Does Mortuary Variability in the Ohio Valley Middle Woodland Mean?," *Southeastern Archaeology,* 33(2), pp. 143–152.

Cobb, C. R. (2003) "Mississippian Chiefdoms: How Complex?" *Annual Review of Anthropology* 32(1): 63–84.

Cobb, C. R. and Butler, B. M. (2002) "The Vacant Quarter Revisited: Late Mississippian Abandonment of the Lower Ohio Valley," *American Antiquity,* 67(4), pp. 625–641.

Cobb, C. R. and King, A. (2005) "Re-Inventing Mississippian Tradition at Etowah, Georgia," *Journal of Archaeological Method and Theory,* 12(3), pp. 167–193.

Collins, J. M. (1990) *The Archaeology of the Cahokia Mounds ICT-II: Site Structure.* Springfield: Illinois State Museum (Illinois Historic Preservation Agency, 10).

Cowan, F. L. (2006) "A Mobile Hopewell? Questioning Assumptions of Ohio Hopewell Sedentism," in Charles, D. and Buikstra, J. (eds.), *Recreating Hopewell.* Gainesville: University Press of Florida, pp. 26–49.

Dalan, R. A. *et al.* (2003) *Envisioning Cahokia: A Landscape Perspective.* Dekalb: Northern Illinois University Press.

Dan-Cohen, T. (2017) "Epistemic artefacts: on the uses of complexity in anthropology" *Journal of the Royal Anthropological Institute"* 23(2): 285–301.

Dancey, W. S. (2005). "The Enigmatic Hopewell of the Eastern Woodlands" *North American Archaeology,* 108–137.

Dan-Cohen, T. (2020) "Tracing Complexity: the Case of Archaeology" *American Anthropologist* 122(3): 733–744.

Dancey, W. S. and Pacheco, P. J. (1997) *Ohio Hopewell Community Organization.* Kent, OH: Kent State University Press.

Dawdy, Shannon Lee (2010) Clockpunk Anthropology and the Ruins of Modernity. *Current Anthrpopology* 51(6): 761–793.

De Certeau, M. (2011) *The Practice of Everyday Life. Translated by S. Rendall.* Berkeley: University of California Press.

De Coulanges, F. (1864) *The Ancient City: A Study on the Religion, Law, and Institutions of Greece and Rome.* Boston, MA: Lee and Shephard.

De Munck, B. (2017) "Disassembling the City: A Historical and an Epistemological View on the Agency of Cities," *Journal of Urban History,* 43(5), pp. 811–829.

Deleuze, G. and Guattari, F. (1988) *A Thousand Plateaus.* Minneapolis: University of Minnesota Press.

Deloria Jr., V. (2003) *God is Red.* Golden, CO: Fulcrum.

Deloria Jr., V. (1988) *Custer Died for Your Sins: an Indian Manifesto.* University of Oklahoma Press, Norman.

Deloria Jr., V. (1992) "Indians, Archaeologists, and the Future," *American Antiquity,* 57(4), p. 595.

Descola, P. (2013) *Beyond Nature and Culture.* Chicago, IL: University of Chicago Press.

Dickens, C. (1987) *American Notes and Pictures from Italy.* Oxford: Oxford University Press.

Earle, T. K. (1987) "Chiefdoms in Archaeological and Ethnohistorical Perspective," *Annual Review of Anthropology,* 16, pp. 279–308.

Emerson, T. E. (1997) *Cahokia and the Archaeology of Power.* Tuscaloosa: University of Alabama Press.

Emerson, T. E. (2018) "Greater Cahokia-Chiefdom, State, or City? Urbanism in the North American Midcontinent, AD 1050–1250," in Emerson, T. E., Brennan, T. K., and Koldehoff, B. H. (eds.), *Revealing Greater Cahokia, North America's First Native City: Rediscovery and Large-Scale Excavations of the East St. Louis Precinct.* Champaign: University of Illinois Press (Illinois State Archaeological Survey Series, 12), pp. 487–535.

Emerson, Thomas E., and Kristin Hedman (2016) " The dangers of diversity: the consolidation and dissolution of Cahokia, native North America's first urban polity" in *Beyond Collapse: Archaeological Perspectives on Resilience, Revitalization, and Transformation in Complex Societies,* edited by Ronald K. Faulseit. Center for Archaeological Investigations Occasional Paper No. 42, pp. 147-178. Southern Illinois University: Carbondale.

Emerson, T. E. *et al.* (2020) "Isotopic Confirmation of the Timing and Intensity of Maize Consumption in Greater Cahokia," *American Antiquity,* 85(2), pp. 241–262.

Emerson, T. E. and Hargrave, E. (2000) "Strangers in Paradise? Recognizing Ethnic Mortuary Diversity on the Fringes of Cahokia," *Southeastern Archaeology*, 19(1), pp. 1–23.

Emerson, T. E. and Hughes, R. E. (2000) "Figurines, Flint Clay Sourcing, the Ozark Highlands and Cahokian Acquisition," *American Antiquity*, 65, pp. 79–101.

Ethridge, R. and Bowne, E. E. (eds.) (2020) *The Historical Turn in Southeastern Archaeology*. Gainesville: University of Florida Press.

Feinman, G. (2012) "Circumscription Theory and Political Change: From Determinism to Mechanism and Parameters." *Social Evolution and History* 11(2): 44–47.

Feinman, G. and Neitzel, J. (1984) "Too Many Types: An Overview of Sedentary Prestate Societies in the Americas," *Advances in Archaeological Method and Theory*, pp. 39–102.

Finley, M. I. (1987) "The City," *Opus*, 6–8, pp. 259–321.

Flannery, K. V. (1972) "The Cultural Evolution of Civilizations," *Annual Review of Ecology and Systematics*, 3(1), pp. 399–426.

Fortier, A. C. (2007) *The Archaeology of the East St. Louis Mound Center, Part II: The Northside Excavations*. Urbana: University of Illinois (Transportation Archaeological Research Reports).

Fortier, A. C. and McElrath, D. L. (2002) "Deconstructing the Emergent Mississippian Concept: The Case for the Terminal Late Woodland in the American Bottom," *Midcontinental Journal of Archaeology*, 27, pp. 171–215.

Fowler, Chris (2013) *The Emergent Past: A Relational Realist Archaeology of Early Bronze Age Mortuary Practices*. Oxford University Press: Oxford.

Fowler, M. R. (1997) *The Cahokian Atlas: A Historical Atlas of Cahokia Archaeology*. Revised ed. Urbana: University of Illinois Press (Studies in Archaeology, 2).

Fowler, M. R. *et al.* (1999) *The Mounds 72 Area: Dedicated and Sacred Space in Early Cahokia*. Springfield: Illinois State Museum (Illinois State Museum Reports of Investigations, 54).

Fowles, S. (2013) *An Archaeology of Doings: Secularism and the Study of Pueblo Religion*. Santa Fe, NM: School for Advanced Research Press.

Fried, M. (1967) *The Evolution of Political Society: An Evolution in Political Anthropology*. New York: Random House:.

Fritz, G. J. (2019) *Feeding Cahokia: Early Agriculture in the North American Heartland*. Tuscaloosa: University of Alabama Press.

Gibson, J. L. (2001) *The Ancient Mounds of Poverty Point: Place of Rings*. Gainesville: University Press of Florida.

Gibson, J. L. (2007) "'Formed from the Earth at That Place': The Material Side of Community at Poverty Point," *American Antiquity*, 72(3), pp. 509–523.

Giles, B. T. (2010) "Sacrificing Complexity: Renewal through Ohio Hopewell Rituals," in Alt, S. M. (ed.), *Ancient Complexities: New Perspectives in Precolumbian North America*. Salt Lake City: University of Utah Press, pp. 73–95.

Goldstein, L. G. (2015) *Aztalan Excavations: Work on the Gravel Knoll and West of the Palisade*. East Lansing: Consortium for Archaeological Research, Michigan State University.

Goldstein, L. G. and Freeman, J. (1997) "Aztalan-A Middle Mississippian Village," *The Wisconsin Archaeologist*, 78(1 and 2), pp.223–248.

Goldstein, L. G. and Richards, J. D. (1991) "Ancient Aztalan: The Cultural and Ecological Context of a Late Prehistoric Site in the Midwest," in Emerson, T. E. and Lewis, R. B. (eds.), *Cahokia and the Hinterlands*. Urbana: University of Illinois Press, pp. 193–206.

Gosden, C. (1999) *Anthropology and Archaeology: A Changing Relationship*. New York: Routledge.

Hamilakis, Y. (2013) *Archaeology and the Senses: Human Experience, Memory, and Affect*. Cambridge: Cambridge University Press.

Hamilton, F. E. (1999) "Southeastern Archaic Mounds: Examples of Elaboration in a Temporally Fluctuating Environment?," *Journal of Anthropological Archaeology*, 18(3), pp. 344–355.

Haraway, D. (2007) *When Species Meet*. Minneapolis: University of Minnesota Press.

Harris, O. J. T. (2018) "More than Representation: Multiscalar Assemblages and the Deleuzian Challenge to Archaeology," *History of the Human Sciences*, 31(3), pp. 83–104.

Hays, C. T. and R. A. Weinstein (2010) "Tchefuncte and early woodland." *Archaeology of Louisiana,* 97-119.

Hedman, K. M. *et al.* (2018) "Expanding the Strontium Isoscape for the American Midcontinent: Identifying Potential Places of Origins for Cahokia and Pre-Columbian Migrants," *Journal of Archaeological Science: Reports*, 22, pp. 202–213.

Heidegger, M. (1953, reprint 1996) *Being and Time*. Albany: State University of New York Press.

Henry, E. R. (2017) "Building Bundles, Building Memories: Processes of Remembering in Adena-Hopewell Societies of Eastern North America," *Journal of Archaeological Method and Theory*, 24(1), pp. 188–228.

Henry, E. R. (2018) *Earthen Monuments and Social Movements in Eastern North America: Adena-Hopewell Enclosures on Kentucky's Bluegrass Landscape*. Published PhD Dissertation. Washington University.

Henry, E. R. *et al.* (2017) "Tetrahedron Baked-Clay Objects from An Early Woodland Context at the Jaketown Site, Mississippi," *Southeastern Archaeology*, 36(1), pp. 34–45.

Henry, E. R. *et al.* (2020a) "Beyond Never-Never Land: Integrating LiDAR and Geophysical Surveys at the Johnston Site, Pinson Mounds State Archaeological Park, Tennessee, USA," *Remote Sensing*, 12(15), p. 2364.

Henry, E. R. and Barrier, C. R. (2016) "The Organization of Dissonance in Adena-Hopewell Societies of Eastern North America," *World Archaeology*, 48(1), pp. 87–109.

Henry, E. R., Mickelson, A. M., and Mickelson, M. E. (2020b) "Documenting Ceremonial Situations and Institutional Change at Middle Woodland Geometric Enclosures in Central Kentucky," *Midcontinental Journal of Archaeology*, 45(3), pp. 203–225.

Henry, E. R. and Miller, G. L. (2020) "Toward a Situational Approach to Understanding Middle Woodland Societies in the North American Midcontinent," *Midcontinental Journal of Archaeology*, 45(3), pp. 187–202.

Hilgeman, S. L. (1991) "Angel Negative Painted Design Structure," *Midcontinental Journal of Archaeology*, 16, pp. 3–33.

Hilgeman, S. L. (2000) *Pottery and Chronology at Angel*. Tuscaloosa: University of Alabama Press.

Hively, R. and Horn, R. (2013) "A New and Extended Case for Lunar (and Solar) Astronomy at the Newark Earthworks," *Midcontinental Journal of Archaeology*, 38(1), pp. 83–118.

Hively, R. and Horn, R. (2019) "Hopewell Topography, Geometry, and Astronomy in the Hopewell Core," in Redmond, B. G., Ruby, B. J., and Burks, J. D. (eds.), *Encountering Hopewell in the Twenty-First Century, Ohio and Beyond*. Akron, OH: University of Akron Press, pp. 117–153.

Hively, R. and Howey, M. C. L. (2012) *Mound Builders and Monument Makers of the Northern Great Lakes, 1200–1600*. Norman: University of Oklahoma Press.

Hodder, I. (2010) *Religion and the Emergence of Civilization: Catalhoyuk as a Case Study*. Cambridge: Cambridge University Press.

Hornborg, A. (2006) "Animism, Fetishism, and Objectivism as Strategies for Knowing (or Not Knowing) the World," *Ethnos*, 71(1), pp. 21–32.

Howey, M.C.L. (2012) *Mound Builders and Monument Makers of the Northern Great Lakes, 1200-1600*. University of Oklahoma Press: Normal.

Hoxie, F. E. (2008) "Retrieving the Red Continent: Settler Colonialism and the History of American Indians in the US," *Ethnic and Racial Studies*, 31(6), pp. 1153–1167.

Hudson, C. (1976) *The Southeastern Indians*. Knoxville: University of Tennessee Press.

Hudson, C. (1998) *Knights of Spain, Warriors of the Sun: Hernando de Soto and the South's Ancient Chiefdoms*. Athens: University of Georgia Press.

Hudson, C. *et al.* (1985) "Coosa: A Chiefdom in the Sixteenth-Century Southeastern United States," *American Antiquity*, 50(4), p. 16.

Ingold, T. (1993) "The Temporality of the Landscape," *World Archaeology*, 25 (2), pp. 152–174.

Ingold, T. (2000) *The Perception of the Environment: Essays in Livelihood, Dwelling, and Skill*. London: Routledge.

Ingold, T. (2007) "Materials against Materiality," *Archaeological Dialogues*, 14 (1), pp. 1–16.

Ingold, T. (2012) "Toward an Ecology of Materials," *Annual Review of Anthropology*, 41(1), pp. 427–442.

Ingold, T. (2015) *The Life of Lines*. New York: Routledge.

Irwin, L. (1994) "Dreams, Theory, and Culture: The Plains Vision Quest Paradigm," *American Indian Quarterly*, 18(2), p. 229.

Iseminger, W. (2010) *Cahokia Mounds: America's First City*. Charleston, SC: The History Press.

Jackson, H. E. (1991) "The Trade Fair in Hunter-Gatherer Interaction: The Role of Intersocietal Trade in the Evolution of Poverty Point Culture," in Gregg, S. A. (ed.), *Between Bands and States*. Carbondale: Southern Illinois University (Center for Archaeological Investigations, 9), pp. 265–286.

Jenkins, N. J. (2003) "The Terminal Late Woodland/Mississippian Transition in West and Central Alabama," *Journal of Alabama Archaeology*, 49(1–2), pp. 1–62.

Jones, A. (2012) *Prehistoric Materialities: Becoming Material in Prehistoric Britain and Ireland*. Oxford: Oxford University Press.

Jones, A. M. and Alberti, B. (2013) "Archaeology after Interpretation," in *Archaeology after Interpretation: Returning Materials to Archaeological Theory*, edited by B. Alberti, A.M. Jones, and J. Pollard. Walnut Creek, CA: Left Coast Press, pp. 15–35.

Kassabaum, M. C. (2019) "Early Platforms, Early Plazas: Exploring the Precursors to Mississippian Mound- and-Plaza Centers," *Journal of Archaeological Research*, 27(2), pp. 187–247.

Kassabaum, M. C. (2021) *On Elevated Ground: The History of Platform Mound Ceremonialism in Eastern North America*. Gainesville: University Press of Florida.

Kelly, J. E. (1980) *Formative Developments at Cahokia and the Adjacent American Bottom: A Merrell Tract Perspective*. Published PhD Dissertation. University of Wisconsin.

Kelly, J. E. (1990) "Range Site Community Patterns and the Mississippian Emergence," in Smith, B. D. (ed.), *The Mississippian Emergence*. Washington, DC: Smithsonian Institution Press, pp. 67–112.

Kelly, J. E. (1994) "The Archaeology of the East St. Louis Mound Center: Past and Present," *Illinois Archaeology*, 6(1 and 2), pp. 1–57.

Kelly, J. E. (2000) "The Nature and Context of Emergent Mississippian Cultural Dynamics in the Greater American Bottom," in *Late Woodland Societies: Tradition and Transformation Across the Midcontinent*, edited by T. E. Emerson, and D. McElrath. Lincoln: University of Nebraska Press, pp. 163–175.

Kidder, T. R. (2002) "Mapping Poverty Point," *American Antiquity*, 67(1), pp. 89–101.

Kidder, T. R. and Sassaman, K. E. (2009) "The View from the Southeast," in Emerson, T. E., McElrath, D. L., and Fortier, A. C. (eds.), *Archaic Societies: Diversity and Complexity Across the Midcontinent*. Albany: State University of New York Press, pp. 667–694.

Kidder, T. R. and Sherwood, S. C. (2017) "Look to the Earth: The Search for Ritual in the Context of Mound Construction," *Archaeological and Anthropological Sciences*, 9(6), pp. 1077–1099.

Kimmerer, R. W. (2013) *Braiding Sweetgrass: Indigenous Wisdom, Scientific Knowledge, and the Teachings of Plants*. Minneapolis, MN: Milkweed Editions.

King, A. (2003). *Etowah: The Political History of a Chiefdom Capital*. Tuscaloosa: University of Alabama Press.

King, A. (2012) "Mississippian in the Deep South: Common Themes in Varied Histories," in Pauketat, T. R. (ed.), *The Oxford Handbook of North American Archaeology*. Oxford: Oxford University Press, pp. 509–522.

Knight, V. J. (ed.) (2009) *The Search for Mabila: The Decisive Battle between Hernando de Soto and Chief Tascalusa*. Tuscaloosa: University of Alabama Press.

Knight, V. J. and Steponaitis, V. P. (2006) "A New History of Moundville," in Knight, V. J. and Steponaitis, V. P. (eds.), *Archaeology of the Moundville Chiefdom*. Tuscaloosa: University of Alabama Press, pp. 1–25.

Kolodny, A. (2003) "Fictions of American Prehistory: Indians, Archeology, and National Origin Myths," *American Literature*, 75(4), pp. 693–721.

Koselleck, R. (2004) *Futures Past: on the Semantics of Historical Time.* Columbia University Press: New York, New York.

Krupat, A. (1995) "American Histories, Native American Narratives," *Early American Literature* 30(2): 1165–174.

Krus, A. M. (2016) "The Timing of Precolumbian Militarization in the US Midwest and Southeast," *American Antiquity*, 81(2), pp. 375–388.

Kuttruff, C. (1997) "Louisiana's Lost Heritage: The Monte Sano Mounds," *Louisiana Archaeology Conservancy*, 7(2), pp. 4–6.

Lankford, G. (2007) *Reachable Stars: Patterns in the Ethnoastronomy of Eastern North America.* Tuscaloosa: University of Alabama Press.

Lapham, Increase (1855) *The Antiquities of Wisconsin.* Smithsonian Institution.

Latour, B. (1993) *We Have Never Been Modern.* Boston, MA: Harvard University Press.

Latour, B. (2005) *Reassembling the Social: An Introduction to Actor-Network Theory.* Oxford: Oxford University Press.

LeFevre, Tate A. (2015) *Settler Colonialism in Oxford Bibliographies in Anthropology*, edited by John Jackson. Oxford Press, New York. NP.

Lepper, B. T. (2004) "The Newark Earthworks: Monumental Geometry and Astronomy at a Hopewellian Pilgrimage Center," in Townsend, R. F. and Sharp, R. V. (eds.), *Hero, Hawk, and Open Hand: American Indian Art of the Ancient Midwest and South.* New Haven, CT: Art Institute of Chicago and Yale University Press, pp. 73–81.

Lepper, B. T. (2006) "The Great Hopewell Road and the Role of Pilgrimage in the Hopewell Interaction Sphere," in Charles, D. and Buikstra, J. (eds.), *Recreating Hopewell.* Gainesville: University of Press Florida, pp. 122–133.

Lopinot, N. H. (1992) "Spatial and Temporal Variability in Mississippian Subsistence: The Archaeobotanical Record," in Woods, W. (ed.), *Late Prehistoric Agriculture: Observations from the Midwest*, pp. 44–94. Springfield: Illinois Historic Preservation Agency (Studies in Illinois Archaeology, 8).

Lynott, M. (2015) *Hopewell Ceremonial Landscapes of Ohio: More than Mounds and Geometric Earthworks.* Oxford: Oxbow Books.

Maile, D.U. (2017) "Going Native: South Park Satire, Settler Colonialism, and Hawaiian Indigeneity" *Cultural Studies, Critical Methodologies* 17(1): 60–66.

Marquardt, W. H. (2010) "Shell Mounds in the Southeast: Middens, Monuments, Temple Mounds, Rings, or Works?," *American Antiquity*, 75 (3), pp. 551–570.

Marquardt, W. H. and Watson, P. J. (eds.) (2005) *Archaeology of the Middle Green River Region, Kentucky.* Gainesville: University Press of Florida.

Martinez, D. R. (2006) "Overcoming Hindrances to Our Enduring Responsibility to the Ancestors: Protecting Traditional Cultural Places," *American Indian Quarterly*, 30(3/4), pp. 486–503.

McElrath, D. L., Emerson, T. E., and Fortier, A. C. (2000) "Social Evolution or Social Response? A Fresh Look at the 'Good Gray Cultures' after Four Decades of Midwest Research," in Emerson, T. E., McElrath, D. L., and Fortier, A. C. (eds.), *Late Woodland Societies: Tradition and Transformation Across the Midcontinent*. Lincoln: University of Nebraska Press, pp. 3–36.

Miller, G. L. (2020) "Bladelets and Middle Woodland Situations in Southern Ohio," *Midcontinental Journal of Archaeology*, 45(3), pp. 226–242.

Milner, G. R. (1998) *The Cahokian Chiefdom: The Archaeology of a Mississippian Society*. Washington, DC: Smithsonian Institution Press.

Milner, G. R., Chaplin, G., and Zavodny, E. (2013) "Conflict and Societal Change in Late Prehistoric Eastern North America," *Evolutionary Anthropology: Issues, News, and Reviews*, 22, pp. 96–102.

Monaghan, G. W. *et al.* (2013) "Mound Construction Chronology at Angel Mounds Episodic Mound Construction and Ceremonial Events," *Midcontinental Journal of Archaeology*, 38(2), pp. 155–170.

Monaghan, G. W. and Peebles, C. S. (2010) "The Construction, Use, and Abandonment of Angel Site Mound A Tracing the History of a Middle Mississippian Town through Its Earthworks," *American Antiquity*, 75(4), pp. 935–953.

Moore, C. R. and Thompson, V. D. (2012) "Animism and Green River Persistent Places: A Dwelling Perspective of the Shell Mound Archaic," *Journal of Social Archaeology*, 12(2), pp. 264–284.

Morse, D. F. and Morse, P. A. (1983) *Archaeology of the Central Mississippi Valley*. New York: Academic Press.

Munoz, S. E. *et al.* (2014) "A Record of Sustained Prehistoric and Historic Land Use from the Cahokia Region, Illinois, USA," *Geology*, 42(6), pp. 499–502.

Munoz, S. E. *et al.* (2015) "Cahokia's Emergence and Decline Coincided with Shifts of Flood Frequency on the Mississippi River," *Proceedings of the National Academy of Sciences*, 112(20), pp. 6319–6324.

Murray, Tim (2008) The History, Philosophy, and Sociology of Archaeology: The Case of the Ancient Monuments Protection Act (1882). In *Histories of Archaeology: a Reader in the History Archaeology* edited by, Tim Murray and Christopher Evans. Oxford Scholarship Online: Oxford. NP.

Nassaney, M. S. (1994) "The Historical and Archaeological Context of Plum Bayou Culture in Central Arkansas," *Southeastern Archaeology*, 13(1), pp. 36–55.

Ohnuki-Tierney, E. (1990) *Culture through Time: Anthropological Approaches*. Stanford, CA: Stanford University Press.

Olsen, B. (2010) *In Defense of Things: Archaeology and the Ontology of Objects*. Lanham, MD: Alta Mira Press.

Olsen, B. (2012) "After Interpretation: Remembering Archaeology," *Current Swedish Archaeology*, 20, pp. 11–34.

Ortman, S. G. *et al.* (2014) "The Pre-History of Urban Scaling," *PLOS ONE*. Edited by S. Shennan, 9(2), p. e87902.

Ortmann, A. L. (2010) "Placing the Poverty Point Mounds in their Temporal Context," *American Antiquity*, 75(3), pp. 657–678.

Ortmann, A. L. and Kidder, T. R. (2012) "Building Mound A at Poverty Point, Louisiana: Monumental Public Architecture, Ritual Practice, and Implications for Hunter-Gatherer Complexity," *Geoarchaeology*, 28(1), pp. 66–86.

Pacheco, P. J., J. Burks, and D. Wymer (2020). "Vol. 2 Ch. 3 Ohio Hopewell Settlements on Brown's Bottom." *Encountering Hopewell in the Twenty-First Century, Ohio and Beyond*. The Univeristy of Akron Press: Akron, pp. 71–123.

Papailias, Penelope (2005).*Genres of Recollection: Archival Poetics and Modern Greece*. Palgrave MacMillan: New York, New York.

Pauketat, R., Alt, M., and Kruchten, D. (2015) "City of Earth and Wood: New Cahokia and Its Material-Historical Implications," in Yoffee, N. (ed.), *The Cambridge World History Volume III: Early Cities in Comparative Perspective, 4000 BCE–1200 CE*. Cambridge: Cambridge University Press, p. 11.

Pauketat, T.R. (2001) "Practice and History in Archaeology: An Emerging Paradigm,'" *Anthropological Theory*, 1(1), pp. 73–98.

Pauketat, T. R. (1994) *The Ascent of Chiefs: Cahokia and the Mississippian Politics in Native North America*. Tuscaloosa: University of Alabama Press.

Pauketat, T. R. (1998) "Refiguring the Archaeology of Greater Cahokia," *Journal of Archaeological Research*, 6(1), pp. 45–89.

Pauketat, T. R. (2002) "A Fourth-Generation Synthesis of Cahokia and Mississippianization," *Midcontinental Journal of Archaeology*, 27(2), pp. 149–170.

Pauketat, T. R. (2003) "Resettled Farmers and the Making of a Mississippian Polity," *American Antiquity*, 68(1), pp. 39–66.

Pauketat, T. R. (2004) *Ancient Cahokia and the Mississippians*. Cambridge: Cambridge University Press.

Pauketat, T. R. (2005) *The Archaeology of the East St. Louis Mound Center: Part 1- the Southside Excavations. ISAS Research Reports Volume 21*. Illinois State Archaeological Survey: Urbana.

Pauketat, T. R. (2007) *Chiefdoms and Other Archaeological Delusions.* New York: AltaMira Press.

Pauketat, T. R. (2008) "Founders' Cults and the Archaeology of Wa-kan-da," in Mills, B. J. and Walker, W. H. (eds.), *Memory Work: The Archaeologies of Material Practice.* Santa Fe, NM: School for Advanced Research Press, pp. 61–80.

Pauketat, T. R. (2009) *Cahokia: Ancient America's Great City on the Mississippi.* New York: Penguin.

Pauketat, T. R. (2013a) *An Archaeology of the Cosmos: Rethinking Agency and Religion in Ancient America.* London: Routledge.

Pauketat, T. R. (2013b) "Bundles of/in/as Time," in Robb, J. and Pauketat, T. R. (eds.), *Big Histories, Human Lives: Tackling Problems of Scale in Archaeology,* pp. 35–56. Santa Fe, NM: School for Advanced Research Press (School for Advanced Research Advanced Seminar Series).

Pauketat, T. R. (2017) "Illuminating Triangulations: Moonlight and the Mississippian World," in C. Papadopoulos and H. Moyes (eds.) *The Oxford Handbook of Light in Archaeology,* pp. 207–224. Oxford: Oxford University Press.

Pauketat, T. R. (2018) "In and Around Cemetery Mound: The Northside and Southside Excavations at the East St. Louis Precinct," in Emerson, T. E., Koldehoff, B. H., and Brennan, T. K. (eds.), *Revealing Greater Cahokia, North America's First Native City: Rediscovery and Large-Scale Excavations of the East St. Louis Precinct,* pp. 127–146. Urbana-Champaign: University of Illinois Press (Studies in Archaeology).

Pauketat, T. R. (2019) "Fragile Cahokia and Chacoan Orders and Infrastructures," in Yoffee, N. (ed.), *The Evolution of Fragility: Setting the Terms.* Cambridge: McDonald Institute for Archaeological Research University of Cambridge, pp. 89–108.

Pauketat, T. R. (2020a) "What Constituted Cahokian Urbanism?," in Farhat, G. and Dumbarton Oaks (eds.), *Landscapes of Preindustrial Urbanism. Dumbarton Oaks Colloquium on the History of Landscape Architecture,* pp. 89–114. Washington, DC: Dumbarton Oaks Research Library and Collection.

Pauketat, T. R. (2020b) "When the Rains Stopped: Evapotranspiration and Ontology at Ancient Cahokia," *Journal of Anthropological Research,* 76 (4):410–438.

Pauketat, T. R. *et al.* (2015) "An American Indian City," in Pauketat, T. R. and Alt, S. M. (eds.), *Medieval Mississippians: The Cahokian World.* Santa Fe, NM: School for Advanced Research Press, pp. 21–31.

Pauketat, T. R. and Alt S. M. (2015) *Medieval Mississippians: The Cahokian World.* School For Advanced Research Press: Santa Fe, NM.

Pauketat, T. R. and Alt, S. M. (2017) *"Water and Shells in Bodies and Pots: Mississippian Rhizome, Cahokian Poesies,"* in Harrison-Buck, E. and Hendon, J. (eds.), *Relational Identities and Other-than-Human Agency in Archaeology*, pp. 72–99. Boulder: University of Colorado Press.

Pauketat, T. R., Alt, S. M., and Kruchten, J. D. (2017a) "The Emerald Acropolis: Elevating the Moon and Water in the Rise of Cahokia," *Antiquity*, 91(355), pp. 207–222.

Pauketat, T. R., Boszhardt, R. F., and Benden, D. M. (2015a) "Trempealeau Entanglements: An Ancient Colony's Causes and Effects," *American Antiquity*, 80(2), pp. 260–289.

Pauketat, T. R., Boszhardt, R. F., and Kolb, M. (2017b) "Trempealeau's Little Bluff: An Early Cahokian Terraformed Landmark in the Upper Mississippi Valley," *Midcontinental Journal of Archaeology*, 42(2), pp. 168–199.

Pauketat, T. R., Killebrew, A. E., and Micheau, F. (2015b) "Imagined Cities," in N. Yoffee (ed.) *Early Cities in Comparative Perspective, 4000 BCE–1200 CE*. Cambridge: Cambridge University Press, pp. 455–466.

Pauketat, T. R. and Lopinot, N. H. (1997) "Cahokian Population Dynamics," in Pauketat, T. R. and Emerson, T. E. (eds.), *Cahokia: Domination and Ideology in the Mississippian World*. Lincoln: University of Nebraska Press, pp. 103–123.

Pauketat, T. R. and Sassaman, K. E. (2020) *The Archaeology of Ancient North America*. Cambridge: Cambridge University Press.

Peebles, C. S. (1971) "Moundville and Surrounding Sites: Some Structural Considerations of Mortuary Practices," in Brown, J. A. (ed.), *Approaches to the Social Dimension of Mortuary Practices*. Washington, DC: Society for American Archaeology (Memoir 15), pp. 68–91.

Peebles, C. S. (1978) "Determinants of Settlement Size and Location in the Moundville Phase," in Smith, B. D. (ed.), *Mississippian Settlement Patterns*. New York: Academic Press, pp. 369–416.

Peregrine, P. N. (2020) "Climate and Social Change at the Start of the Late Antique Little Ice Age," *The Holocene*, 30(11), pp. 1643–1648.

Peterson, S. A. (2010) *Townscape Archaeology at Angel Mounds*. Published PhD Dissertation. Indiana University.

Pe'tursdo'ttir, P. (2013) Concrete Matters: Ruins of modernity and the things called heritage. *Journal of Social Archaeology* 13(1): 31–53.

Pe'tursdo'ttir, P. and Olsen, B. (2014) "An Archaeology of Ruins," in Olsen, B. and P. Pe'tursdo'ttir (eds.) *Ruin Memories: Materiality, Aesthetics and the Archaeology of the Recent Past*. New York: Routledge, pp. 3–30.

Phillips, P. (1970) *Archaeological Survey in the Lower Yazoo Basin, Mississippi, 1949–1955*. Cambridge, MA: Harvard University Press (Papers of the Peabody Museum of Archaeology and Ethnology, 60).

Povinelli, E. (2016) *Geontologies: A Requiem to Late Liberalism*. Durham, NC: Duke University Press.

Price, T. D., Burton, J. H., and Stoltman, J. B. (2007) "Place of Origin of Prehistoric Inhabitants of Aztalan, Jefferson Co., Wisconsin," *American Antiquity*, 72(3), pp. 524–538.

Pursell, C. O. (2013) "Colored Monuments and Sensory Theater among the Mississippians," in J. Day (ed.) *Making Sense of the Past: Toward a Sensory Archaeology*. Edwardsville: Southern Illinois University Press (Center for Archaeological Investigations, Occasional Paper No. 40), pp. 69–89.

Railey, J. A. (1991) "Woodland Settlement Trends and Symbolic Architecture in the Kentucky Bluegrass," in Stout, C. and Hensley, C. K. (eds.), *The Human Landscape in Kentucky's Past: Site Structure and Settlement Patterns*. Frankfort: Kentucky Heritage Council, pp. 56–77.

Randall, A. R. (2013) "The Chronology and History of Mount Taylor Period (ca. 7400–4600 cal BP) Shell Sites on the Middle St. Johns River, Florida, " *Southeastern Archaeology*, 32(2), pp. 193–217.

Randall, A. R. and Sassaman, K. (2017) "Terraforming the Middle Ground in Ancient Florida," *Hunter Gatherer Research*, 3(1), pp. 9–29.

Rees, M. A. and Lee, A. L. (2015) "On the Monumentality of Events: Refiguring Late Woodland Culture History at Troyville," in Gilmore, Z. I. and O'Donoughue, J. (eds.), *The Archaeology of Events: Cultural Change and Continuity in the Pre-Columbian Southeast*. Tuscaloosa: University of Alabama Press, pp. 160–195.

Regnier, A. L. (2014) *Reconstructing Tascalusa's Chiefdom: Pottery Styles and the Social Composition of Late Mississippian Communities along the Alabama River*. Tuscaloosa: University of Alabama Press.

Renfrew, C., Todd, I., and Tringham, R. (1974) "Beyond a Subsistence Economy: The Evolution of Social Organization in Prehistoric Europe," *Bulletin of the American Schools of Oriental Research*, (20), pp. 69–95.

Richards, J. D. (1992) *Ceramics and Culture at Aztalan, a Late Prehistoric Village in Southeast Wisconsin*. Published PhD Dissertation. University of Wisconsin.

Richards, J. D. (2007) "Context and Process: Red-Slipped Pottery in Cahokia's Northern Hinterlands," *Illinois Archaeology*, 19, pp. 1–26.

Richards, J. D. and Jeske, R. J. (2002) "Location, Location, Location: The Temporal and Cultural Context of Late Prehistoric Settlement in Southeast Wisconsin," *Wisconsin Archaeologist*, 83(2), pp. 32–54.

Richards, J. D. and Zych, T. (2018) "A Landscape of Mounds: Community Ethnogenesis at Aztalan," in Koldehoff, B. H. and Pauketat, T. R. (eds.),

Archaeology and Ancient Religion in the American Midcontinent. Tuscaloosa: University of Alabama Press, pp. 234–268.

Robb, J. and Pauketat, T. R. (2013) "From Moments to Millennia: Theorizing Scale and Change in Human History," in J. Robb, T. R. Pauketat (eds.) *Big Histories, Human Lives: Tackling Problems of Scale in Archaeology.* Santa Fe, NM: School for Advanced Research Press (School for Advanced Research Advanced Seminar Series), pp. 3–34.

Rolingson, M. A. (1998) *Toltec Mounds and Plum Bayou Culture: Mound D Excavations.* Arkansas Archaeological Survey Research Series, 54. Fayetteville: Arkansas Archaeological Survey.

Romain, W. F. (2000) *Mysteries of the Hopewell: Astronomers, Geometers, and Magicians of the Eastern Woodlands.* Akron, OH: University of Akron Press.

Romain, W. F. (2014) "Ancient Astronomers of the Eastern Woodlands: Watson Brake to Cahokia," in *Midwest Archaeological Conference*, Urbana-Champaign.

Romain, W. F. (2015a) "Moonwatchers of Cahokia," in Pauketat, T. R. and Alt, S. M. (eds.), *Medieval Mississipians: The Cahokian World.* Santa Fe, NM: School for Advanced Research Press, pp. 33–43.

Romain, W. F. (2015b) *An Archaeology of the Sacred: Adena-Hopewell Astrology and Landscape Arcaheology*, Ancient Earthworks Project. NP.

Romain, W. F. (2017) "Monks Mound as an Axis Mundi for the Cahokian World." *Illinois Archaeology* 29(27–52).

Romain, W. F. (2019) "Ancient Skywatchers of the Mississippi Valley," in *Lecture Presented at the Maya Exploration Center*, Chillicothe, OH.

Russo, M. and Heide, G. (2001) "Shell Rings of the Southeast US," *Antiquity*, 75(289), pp. 491–492.

Sampson, K. A. (2008) *Getting to the Point: Typology, Morphology, and Lithic Material Variation in the Milwaukee Public Museum Project Point Collection from the Aztalan Sites.* Published Master's Thesis. University of Wisconsin.

Sanger, M. C. (2015) *Life in the Round: Shell Rings of the Georgie Bight.* Published PhD Dissertation. Columbia University.

Sanger, M. C. *et al.* (2020) "Multiple-Proxy Seasonality Indicators: An Integrative Approach to Assess Shell Midden Formations from Late Archaic Shell Rings in the Coastal Southeast North America," *The Journal of Island and Coastal Archaeology*, 15(3), pp. 333–363.

Sanger, M. C. and Thomas, D. H. (2010) "The Two Rings of St. Catherine's Island: Some Preliminary Results from the St. Catherine's and McQueen Shell Rings," in Thomas, D. H. and Sanger, M. C. (eds.), *Trend, Tradition, and Turmoil: What Happened to the Southeastern Archaic?* American Museum of Natural History Anthropological Papers, 93, pp. 45–70.

Sassaman, K. E. (2004) "Complex Hunter-Gatherers in Evolution and History: A North American Perspective," *Journal of Archaeological Research*, 12(3), pp. 227–280.

Sassaman, K. E. (2005) "Poverty Point as Structure, Event, Process," *Journal of Archaeological Method and Theory*, 12(4), pp. 335–364.

Sassaman, K. E. (2006) *People of the Shoals: Stallings Culture of the Savannah River Valley*. Gainesville: University Press of Florida.

Sassaman, K. E. (2010) *The Eastern Archaic: Historicized*. New York: Alta Mira Press.

Sassaman, K. E. (2016) "A Constellation of Practice in the Experience of Sea-Level Rise," in Roddick, A. and Stahl, A. (eds.), *Knowledge in Motion: Constellations of Learning Across Time and Space*, pp. 271-298. Tucson: University of Arizona Press

Sassaman, K. E., Blessing, M. E., and Randall, A. (2006) "Stallings Island Revisited: New Evidence for Occupational History, Community Pattern, and Subsistence Technology," *American Antiquity*, 71(3), pp. 539–565.

Sassaman, K. and Randall, A. (2012) "Early New World Monumentality," in Burger, E. R. L. and Rosenswig, R. M. (eds.), *Early New World Monumentality*. Gainesville: University Press of Florida, pp. 53–77.

Saunders, J. W. (2004) "Are We Fixing to Make the Same Mistake again?," in Gibson, J. L. and Carr, P. J. (eds.), *Signs of Power: The Rise of Cultural Complexity in the Southeast*, pp. 146–161. Tuscaloosa: University of Alabama Press.

Saunders, J. W. (2010) "Middle Archaic and Watson Brake," in Rees, M. A. (ed.), *Archaeology of Louisiana*. Baton Rouge: Louisiana State University Press, pp. 63–76.

Saunders, J. W. *et al.* (2005) "Watson Brake, a Middle Archaic Mound Complex in Northeast Louisiana," *American Antiquity*, 70(4), pp. 631–668.

Saunders, J. W., Mandel, R. D., and Saucier, R. T. (1997) "A Mound Complex in Louisiana at 5400–5000 Years before Present," *Science*, 277, pp. 1796–1799.

Saunders, R. (1994) "The Case for Archaic Mounds Sites in Southeastern Louisiana," *Southeastern Archaeology*, 13, pp. 118–134.

Saunders, R. (2017) *Archaic Shell Mounds in the American Southeast*. Oxford: Oxford University Press.

Saunders, R. and Russo, M. (2011) "Coastal Shell Middens in Florida: A View from the Archaic Period," *Quaternary International*, 239(1–2), pp. 38–50.

Schilling, T. (2012) "Building Monks Mound, Cahokia, Illinois, A.D. 800–1400," *Journal of Field of Archaeology*, 37(4), pp. 302–313.

Service, E. R. (1962) *Primitive Social Organization: An Evolutionary Perspective*. New York: Random House.

Sherwood, S. C. and Kidder, T. R. (2011) "The DaVincis of Dirt: Geoarchaeological Perspectives on Native American Mound Building in the Mississippi River Basin," *Journal of Anthropological Archaeology*, 30 (1), pp. 69–87.

Shorter, D. D. (2016) *Spirituality*. Edited by F. E. Hoxie. Oxford: Oxford University Press.

Silliman, Stephen (2005) "Culture Contact or Colonialism? Challenges in the Archaeology of Native North America", *American Antiquity* 70(1): 55–74.

Simon, M. L. (2002) "Red Cedar, White Oak, and Bluestem Grass: The Colors of Mississippian Construction, " *Midcontinental Journal of Archaeology*, 27 (2), pp. 273–308.

Silliman, Silliman (2008) *Collaborating at the Trowels Edge: teaching and learning in Indigenous archaeology*. University of Arizona Press: Tucson. Silliman

Simon, M. L. (2014) "Reevaluating the Introduction of Maize into the American Bottom of Southern Illinois," *Occasional Papers Official Publication of the Midwest Archaeological Conference*, 1, pp. 97–134.

Simon, M. L. (2017) "Reevaluating the Evidence for Middle Woodland Maize from the Holding Site," *American Antiquity*, 82(1), pp. 140–150.

Skousen, B. J. (2012a) "Posts as Ancestors: New Insights into Monumental Posts in the American Bottom," *Southeastern Archaeology*, 31, pp. 57–69.

Skousen, B. J. (2012b) "Pots, Places, Ancestors, and Worlds: Dividual Personhood in the American Bottom Region," *Southeastern Archaeology*, 31(1), pp. 57–69.

Slater, Philip A., Kristin Hedman, Thomas E. Emerson (2014) Immigrants at the Mississippian polity of Cahokia: strontium isotope evidence for population movement. *Journal of Archaeological Science*. 44: 117–127.

Smith, L. (2006) *Uses of Heritage*. London: Routledge.

Smith, M. E. (2010) "The Archaeological Study of Neighborhoods and Districts in Ancient Cities," *Journal of Anthropological Archaeology*, 29, pp. 137–154.

Smith, M. L., ed. (2010) *The Social Construction of Ancient Cities*. Smithsonian Institution: Washington, DC.

Smith, M. L. (2014) "The Archaeology of Urban Landscapes," *Annual Review of Anthropology*, 43(1), pp. 307–323.

Smith, M. L. (2020) *Cities: The First 6000 Years*. Penguin Books: New York.

Spivey, S. M. *et al.* (2015) "Pilgrimage to Poverty Point?," in Gilmore, Z. I. and O'Donoughue, J. (eds.), *The Archaeology of Events*. Tuscaloosa: University of Alabama Press, pp. 141–159.

Squier, E. G. and Davis, E. H. (1848) *Ancient Monuments of the Mississippi Valley*. Washington, DC: Smithsonian Institution (Smithsonian Contributions to Knowledge, 1).

Squier, G. H. (1905) "Certain Archaeological Features of Western Wisconsin," *The Wisconsin Archaeologist*, 4, pp. 24–28.

Squier, G. H. (1917) "Archaeology," in Curtiss-Wedge, F. and Pierce, E. D. (eds.), *History of Trempealeau County*. Chicago: H. C. Cooper, Jr., pp. 26–35.

Steponaitis, V. P. (1998) "Population Trends at Moundville," in Knight, V. J. and Steponaitis, V. P. (eds.), *Archaeology of the Moundville Chiefdom*. Washington, DC: Smithsonian Institution Press, pp. 26–43.

Steponaitis, V. P., Kassabaum, M. C., and O'Hear, J. W. (2015) "Cahokia's Cole Creek Predecessors," in Pauketat, T. R. and Alt, S. M. (eds.), *Medieval Mississippians: The Cahokian World*. Santa Fe, NM: School for Advanced Research Press, pp. 13–19.

Stewart, C. (2016) "Historicity and Anthropology," *Annual Review of Anthropology*, 45(1), pp. 79–94.

Struever, S. and Houart, G. L. (1972) "An Analysis of the Hopewell Interaction Sphere," *Social Exchange and Interaction*, 46, pp. 47–79.

TallBear, K. and Willey, A. (2019a) "Introduction: Critical Relationality: Queer, Indigenous, and Multispecies Belonging Beyond Settler Sex & Nature," *Imaginations: Journal of Cross-Cultural Image Studies/revue d'études interculturelle de l'image*, 10(1):5–15

TallBear, K. and Willey, A. (2019b) "Critical Relationality: Queer, Indigenous, and Multispecies Belonging Beyond Settler Sex & Nature," *Imaginations: Journal of Cross-Cultural Image Studies* 10(1), pp. 5–15.

Taylor, P. J. (2012) "Extraordinary Cities: Early 'City-ness' and the Origins of Agriculture and States," *International Journal of Urban and Regional Research*, 36(3), pp. 415–447.

Theler, J. L. and Boszhardt, R. F. (2000) "The End of the Effigy Mound Culture: The Late Woodland to Oneota Transition in Southwestern Wisconsin," *Midcontinental Journal of Archaeology*, 25(2), pp. 289–312.

Thomas, J. (2015) "The Future of Archaeological Theory," *Antiquity*, 89(348), pp. 1287–1296.

Thompson, V. D. (2010) "The rythms of space-time and the making of monuments and places during the Archaic." *Trend, Tradition, and Turmoil: What happened to the Southeastern Archaic* 93: 217–27.

Todd, Z. (2016) "An Indigenous Feminist's Take on the Ontological Turn: 'Ontology' is Just Another Word for Colonialism," *Journal of Historical Sociology*, 29(1), pp. 4–22.

Topping, P. (2010) "Native American Mound Building Traditions," in Leary, J., Darvill, T., and Field, D. (eds.), *Round Mounds and Monumentality in the*

British Neolithic and Beyond. Oxford: Oxbow Books (Neolithic Studies Group Seminar Papers), pp. 219–252.

Trigger, B. G. (1980) "Archaeology and the Image of the American Indian" *American Antiquity* 45(4): 662–676.

Turner, F. J. (1894) *The Significance of the Frontier in American History*. Madison: State Historical Society of Wisconsin.

VanDerwarker, A., Bardolph, D., and Scarry, C. M. (2017) "Maize and Mississippian Beginnings," in Wilson, G. D. (ed.), *Mississippian Beginnings*. Gainesville: University of Florida Press, pp. 29–70.

Verancini, Lorenzo (2013) "'Settler Colonialism': Career of a Concept", *The Journal of Imperial and Commonwealth History* 41(2): 313–333.

Viveiros de Castro, E. (2012) "Cosmological Perspectivism in Amazonia and Elsewhere," *HAU Masterclass Series*, 1, pp. 45–168.

Viveiros de Castro, E. (2014) *Cannibal Metaphysics*. Minneapolis: University of Minnesota Press.

Wallis, N. J. (2011) *The Swift Creek Gift: Vessel Exchange on the Atlantic Coast*. Tuscaloosa: University of Alabama Press.

Watson, P. J. and Kennedy, M. C. (1991) "The Development of Horticulture in the Eastern Woodlands of North America: Women's Roles," in Gero, J. and Conkey, M. (eds.), *Engendering Archaeology: Women and Prehistory*. Oxford: Blackwell, pp. 255–275.

Watts, C. (2013a) *Relational Archaeologies*. New York: Routledge.

Watts, V. (2013b) "Indigenous Place-Thought and Agency amongst Humans and Non-Humans (First Woman and Sky Woman Go on a European World Tour!)," *Decolonization: Indigeneity, Education & Society*, 2(1), pp. 20–34.

Watts Malouchos, E. (2020a) "Angel Ethnogenesis and the Cahokian Diaspora," *Journal of Archaeological Method and Theory*, 27(1), pp. 128–156.

Watts Malouchos, E. (2020b) *Assembling Mississippian Communities: Integration, Identity, and Everyday Practices in the Angel Hinterlands*. Published PhD Dissertation. Indiana University.

Watts Malouchos, E. (2021) "Reconsidering Mississippian Communities and Households," in Watts Malouchos, E. and Betzenhauser, A. (eds.), *Reconsidering Mississippian Communities and Households*. Tuscaloosa: University of Alabama Press, pp. 9–31.

Webb, W. S. (1940) *The Wright Mounds, Sites 6 and 7, Montgomery County, Kentucky*. Lexington: University of Kentucky (University of Kentucky Department of Anthropology, 1).

Webb, W. S. and Baby, R. S. (1957) *The Adena People #2*. Columbus: Ohio Historical Society.

Webb, W. S. and Snow, C. E. (1945) *The Adena People.* Lexington: University of Kentucky.

Welch, D. J. (1975) *Wood Utilization at Cahokia: Identification of Wood Charcoal from the Merrell Tract.* Madison: University of Wisconsin.

Welch, P. D. (2006) *Archaeology at Shiloh Indian Mounds 1899–1999.* Tuscaloosa: University of Alabama Press.

Wesson, C. B. and Rees, M. A. (eds.) (2002) *Between Contacts and Colonies: Archaeological Perspectives on the Protohistoric Southeast.* Tuscaloosa: University of Alabama Press.

White, A.J., S.E. Munoz, S. Schroeder, and L.R. Stevens (2020) "After Cahokia: Indigenous Repopulation and Depopulation of the Horseshoe Lake Watershed AD 1400-1900." *American Antiquity* 85(2): 263–278.

Willey, G. R. and Sabloff, J. A. (1980) *A History of American Archaeology.* 2nd ed. San Francisco, CA: W. H. Freeman.

Wilson, G. D. (2008) *The Archaeology of Everyday Life at Early Moundville.* Tuscaloosa: University of Alabama Press.

Wilson, G. D. (2010) "Community, Identity, and Social Memory at Moundville," *American Antiquity,* 75(1), pp. 3–18.

Wittry, W. L. (1969) "The American Woodhenge," *Explorations into Cahokia Archaeology,* 7:43–48.

Wolfe, Patrick (2006) "Settler colonialism and the elimination of the native", *Journal of Genocide Research* 8(4): 387–409.

Wright, A. P. (2017) "Local and 'Global' Perspectives on the Middle Woodland Southeast," *Journal of Archaeological Research,* 25(1), pp. 37–83.

Wright, A. P. (2020) *Garden Creek: The Archaeology of Interaction in Middle Woodland Appalachia.* Tuscaloosa: University of Alabama Press.

Wright, H. T. (1984) "Prestate Political Formations," in Sanders, W. T. and Wright, H. T. (eds.), *On the Evolution of Complex Societies: Essays in Honor of Harry Hoijer.* Los Angeles, CA: UCLA Department of Anthropology (Other Realities), pp. 41–77.

Wright, H. T. and G. A. Johnson (1975) "Population, Exchange, and Early State Formation in Southwestern Iran." *American Anthropologist* 77(2): 267–289. *Wright*

Yoffee, N. (2009) "Making Ancient Cities Plausible," *Reviews in Anthropology,* 38, pp. 264–289.

Yoffee, N. (2015) "Conclusion: The Meaning of Early Cities," in N. Yoffee (ed.) *Early Cities in Comparative Perspective, 4000 BCE–1200 CE.* Cambridge: Cambridge University Press (The Cambridge World History), pp. 546–557.

Yoffee, N. and Terrenato, N. (2015) "Introduction: A History of the Study of Early Cities," in N. Yofee (ed.) *Early Cities in Comparative Perspective, 4000 BCE–1200 CE*. Cambridge: Cambridge University Press, pp. 1–24.

Zigon, J. (2015) "View of What Is a Situation? An Assemblic Ethnography of the Drug War.," *Cultural Anthropology*, 30, pp. 501–524.

Zych, T. (2015a) "Aztalan's Northeast Mound: The Construction of Community," *The Wisconsin Archaeologist*, 96(2), pp. 53–118.

Zych, T. (2015b) "The Game of Chunkey," in Pauketat, T. R. and Alt, S. M. (eds.), *Medieval Mississippians: The Cahokian World*, pp. 71–74. Santa Fe, NM: School for Advanced Research Press.

Cambridge Elements ☰

The Global Middle Ages

Geraldine Heng
University of Texas at Austin

Geraldine Heng is Perceval Professor of English and Comparative Literature at the University of Texas, Austin. She is the author of *The Invention of Race in the European Middle Ages* (2018) and *England and the Jews: How Religion and Violence Created the First Racial State in the West* (2018), both published by Cambridge, as well as *Empire of Magic: Medieval Romance and the Politics of Cultural Fantasy* (2003, Columbia). She is the editor of *Teaching the Global Middle Ages* (2022, MLA), coedits the University of Pennsylvania Press series, RaceB4Race: Critical Studies of the Premodern, and is working on a new book, Early Globalisms: The Interconnected World, 500–1500 CE. Originally from Singapore, Heng is a fellow of the Medieval Academy of America, a member of the Medievalists of Color, and founder and codirector, with Susan Noakes, of the Global Middle Ages Project: www .globalmiddleages.org

Susan Noakes
University of Minnesota, Twin Cities

Susan Noakes is a professor and chair of French and Italian at the University of Minnesota, Twin Cities. From 2002 to 2008, she was Director of the Center for Medieval Studies; she has also served as Director of Italian Studies, Director of the Center for Advanced Feminist Studies, and Associate Dean for Faculty in the College of Liberal Arts. Her publications include *The Comparative Perspective on Literature: Essays in Theory and Practice* (coedited with Clayton Koelb, Cornell, 1988) and *Timely Reading: Between Exegesis and Interpretation* (Cornell, 1988), along with many articles and critical editions in several areas of French, Italian, and neo-Latin Studies. She is the founder and codirector, with Geraldine Heng, of the Global Middle Ages Project: www.globalmiddleages.org

About the Series

Elements in the Global Middle Ages is a series of concise studies that introduce researchers and instructors to an uncentered, interconnected world, c. 500–1500 CE. Individual Elements focus on the globe's geographic zones, its natural and built environments, and its cultures, societies, arts, technologies, peoples, ecosystems, and lifeworlds.

Cambridge Elements ≡

The Global Middle Ages

Elements in the Series

The Global Middle Ages: An Introduction
Geraldine Heng

The Market in Poetry in the Persian World
Shahzad Bashir

Oceania, 800-1800CE: A Millennium of Interactions in a Sea of Islands
James L. Flexner

Cahokia and the North American Worlds
Sarah E. Baires

A full series listing is available at: www.cambridge.org/EGMA

Printed in the United States
by Baker & Taylor Publisher Services